MEASURING UP

THE BUSINESS CASE FOR GIS

Christopher Thomas and Milton Ospina

ESRI PRESS

REDLANDS, CALIFORNIA

First printing July 2004.

Printed in the United States of America.

Library of Congress Cataloging-in-Publication Data
Thomas, Christopher, 1963 Aug. 6—
Measuring up : the business case for GIS / Christopher Thomas and Milton Ospina.
   p. cm.
  Includes bibliographical references.
  ISBN 1-58948-088-0 (pbk. : alk. paper)
  1. Decision support systems. 2. Geographic information systems. 3. Industrial management. I. Ospina, Milton. II. Title.
HD30.213.T47 2004
658.4'038—dc22   2004013898

Published by ESRI, 380 New York Street, Redlands, California 92373—8100.

Books from ESRI Press are available to resellers worldwide through Independent Publishers Group (IPG). For information on volume discounts, or to place an order, call IPG at 1-800-888-4741 in the United States, or at 312-337-0747 outside the United States.

acknowledgments

Many people played key roles in the development of this book. Dozens of case study authors contributed stories about how GIS benefits their companies, agencies, and communities. Our greatest thanks go to those who excel in making GIS a critical component of their daily business processes and work flow. When we first began to work on this book, we were pleased to discover the many different benefits that come from implementing GIS technology in businesses across the world—how all the book contributors have made a business difference in their place of employment and how they are providing better services and products to their clients, shareholders, and citizens.

From start to finish, Shelley Christensen, ESRI® Government team assistant, has been instrumental in making this book a reality. From tracking, researching, and writing case studies to monitoring authors and completing a multitude of logistical tasks, Shelley has demonstrated great professionalism, and without her support this book would not have been published.

Heartfelt thanks to Nancy Sappington, our ESRI editor, for editorial guidance in making this book the best it could be considering the many different angles and audiences we wanted to address. She edited the book to make the benefits of GIS easy to comprehend and to encourage others to identify the benefits that GIS technology and science bring to their businesses and end users. Thanks also to Sara Bobbitt, who designed the cover, and Cliff Crabbe, who oversaw print production.

Thank you to the numerous ESRI staff members who contributed to this book by providing case study leads, graphics design, and logistical and managerial support. They are Jeff Allen, Ann Bossard, Lee Burton, Buyang Cao, Bill Davenhall, David Davis, Rob Della Marna, Roxanne Cox–Drake, Mike Hyatt, Linda Hecht, Karen Hurlbut, Brenda Martinez, Brad McCallum, Lew Nelson, Steve Trammell, Geoff Wade, and Debbie Wright. Some of the case studies were previously published in the magazines *ArcNews*™ and *ArcUser*™, but were updated to reflect enhanced or new GIS benefits. We thank Tom Miller (*ArcNews* editor) and Monica Pratt (*ArcUser* editor) for their support.

This book would not be a reality were it not for the support of ESRI Press Publisher Christian Harder for giving us the freedom to be creative and to approach this book in our own way. Special thanks to Jack Dangermond, ESRI president, for inspiring us all to make the world a better place through GIS technology.

Finally, we thank the book's contributors—busy and accomplished professionals with many demands on their time. They provided excellent examples of how GIS benefits their business practices and how GIS has had a positive impact on the bottom line. The result is a unique collection of seventy-five case studies representing six industries and twenty-two business sectors. All praises belong to them:

Heather Adams, ESRI Canada Limited; Eliot Allen, Criterion Planners/Engineers, Inc.; Marcy Allen, CommunityViz; Dean Angelides, VESTRA Resources, Inc.; Bill Ballard, City of Baltimore; Manju Book, Arrowhead Credit Union; Nate Boonisar, Norfolk County, Massachusetts; Patrick Bresnahan, PhD, Richland County, South Carolina; William Burnett, California Office of Statewide Health Planning and Development (CA OSHPD); Scott Christman, CA OSHPD; Keith Cooke, Geographic Information Services, Inc.; Pat Egetter, Riverside County, California; Les Greenberg, AOT Public Safety Corporation; Jess Hansen, Anderson & Associates; Katherine Harness, U.S. Department of the Interior, Bureau of Land Management; David Herzog, University of Missouri School of Journalism; Mike Heslin, City of Moreno Valley, California; Ana Hiraldo, Westchester County, New York; Shelby Johnson, State of Arkansas; Richard E. Klosterman, What if?, Inc.; Dave Lawson, Norfolk County, Massachusetts; Paige Medlin, UCLID Software; Dave Michaelson, Gunnison County, Colorado; Chris North, ESRI Canada; Christopher J. Pettit, RMIT University, Melbourne, Australia; Frank Roberts, Coeur d'Alene Tribe; Steve Romalewski, New York Public Interest Research Group Community Mapping Assistance Project; Rosa Rubbo de Carvalho, CADDesign; Julie Seidel, CommunityViz; Jared Shoultz and Murray Hudson, Public Health Statistics and Information Services, South Carolina Department of Health and Environmental Control; Rick Thomas, PartnerRe, Ltd.; Steve Waldron, City of Richmond, Virginia; Chris Walz, RouteSmart Technologies, Inc.; Neal Weinberg, City of Albuquerque, New Mexico; Deb Wong, CA OSHPD; and Feng Yang, Town of Brookline, Massachusetts.

Milton Ospina
ESRI Urban and Regional Planning and Economic Development Solutions Manager

Christopher Thomas
ESRI State and Local Government Solutions Manager

foreword

Geography impacts our daily lives in so many ways, yet most people have not been aware of how they can use geography as a way to organize their world. All that is changing.

For more than three decades, ESRI has been involved in the development of a computer technology known as geographic information systems (GIS), and we are focused on making GIS technology as widely available as possible. GIS tools help us digitize, integrate, analyze, and map geographic layers of information. With GIS, people are examining all types of issues and making better-informed decisions.

Digital maps can readily reveal trends, patterns, and answers to questions not easily apparent with other data presentations, and organizations around the world are extracting more value from their information technology investments by integrating GIS software. GIS is becoming a mainstream solution environment that both complements and makes use of many traditional information technologies.

Measuring Up presents case studies from twenty-two segments of society. The stories tell us not only what people across the globe are doing with GIS, but how GIS has served to improve their communities and organizations. Whether you work in the public or private sector, *Measuring Up* will help you gain insight about how intelligent geographic information systems—digital versions of geography—encapsulate our knowledge and provide a foundation to help us better serve our world by improving efficiencies, decision making, planning, accountability, and communication.

With so many examples in the book from businesses to police departments to utility companies to non-profit organizations, you will be able to see how GIS can be applied to and improve your particular situation.

GIS is revolutionizing how we work and enabling us to concentrate on the information rather than the technology. It has become easier to use, more standardized, and more embedded with mission-critical software applications. *Measuring Up* includes discussion and examples of how GIS can shift from project-specific uses to an enterprise database that supports many kinds of interrelated work flows in organizations.

GIS technology continues to evolve. Geography and GIS can provide enormous benefits to an organization. It also helps us as a society to manage and interact with the environment.

Jack Dangermond
President, ESRI

contents

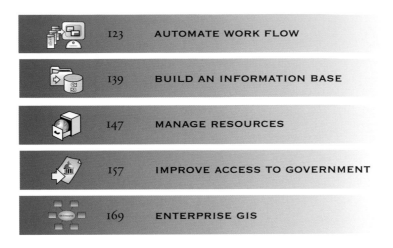

chapter topics/industry matrix

INDUSTRY / SECTOR	Save money/Cost avoidance 1	Save time 21	Increase efficiency 31	Increase accuracy 43	Increase productivity 57	Communication and collaboration 65	Generate revenue 79	Support decision making 91	Aid budgeting 113	Automate work flow 123	Build an information base 139	Manage resources 147	Improve access to government 169
BUSINESS													
Banking and insurance	●							●					
Media				●									
Real estate	●												
GOVERNMENT													
Administration/Management			●				●●	●					●
Cadastral				●							●	●	●
Economic development	●						●						●
Elections								●			●		●
Finance										●●			
Health and human services	●			●		●					●		●
Law enforcement and criminal justice				●		●							
Planning	●	●●	●				●	●●●	●		●●	●	
Public safety		●	●●			●	●	●		●		●	
Public works			●	●●		●						●	
NATURAL RESOURCES													
Agriculture								●					
Forestry					●								
TRANSPORTATION													
Logistics and fleet management	●	●			●								
Transportation systems and networks										●			
UTILITIES													
Electric and gas			●	●				●	●		●	●	
Telecommunication					●								

Legend:
● Not for profit
● International
  Federal
● State
● Regional
● County
● Municipality
● Tribal
● Private industry

introduction

Measuring the benefits of implementing GIS

GIS brings people from disparate groups and different disciplines together and helps them understand problems through a common visual language. GIS has demonstrated real business value, and as a result numerous companies, agencies, and government organizations have established GIS programs during the last thirty years. The case studies documented in this book present the spectrum of benefits—tangible and intangible—that GIS brings to many disciplines and industries.

Many of the featured organizations are realizing a return on investment by integrating GIS into their information systems and maximizing the benefits of GIS by incorporating it into their daily business work flow. Organizations that implement a GIS throughout all business tasks become more efficient, have access to more information, save time and money, and increase productivity as they create and maintain successful customer service programs. Communication improves internally and externally when a company uses a GIS. Maximizing your investment in GIS will lead to increased accuracy and will support the decision-making process within the organization—large or small.

Measuring Up covers thirteen benefits of implementing a GIS. The organizations featured have measured how GIS is making them more productive and efficient, how costs were avoided, and how the use of GIS technology has improved their communication internally and with their customers. The chapter on making the business case for enterprise GIS discusses the basic issues businesses and organizations should consider as they expand their GIS programs to achieve a higher level of benefits. This book shows how GIS can support organizations and businesses and help them realize benefits that include the following:

- saving time
- increasing efficiency
- saving money/avoiding cost
- generating revenue
- providing decision support
- automating work flow

- increasing communication and collaboration
- aiding in budgeting
- building an information base/managing knowledge
- increasing accuracy
- increasing productivity
- managing resources
- improving access to government

GIS is changing the way people view spatial information

In the three decades since the development of GIS technology, thousands of state and local governments, private companies, corporations, and numerous other organizations have benefited from integrating GIS software into their daily operations. The pioneering efforts of the state and local agencies that waded into the uncharted waters of this new science helped to define a vision that today is shared by many other business sectors.

What is the business value of adopting GIS? Initially, some departments saw GIS as an indispensable tool for their discipline, while others implemented GIS to achieve the goals of a specific project. Throughout the development of the technology, organizations have tested the power of GIS to enable them to keep pace with current customer expectations. Increasingly, as these case studies show, organizations are realizing that GIS is a valuable tool to help them move forward efficiently while responding to issues of accountability and performance measurement.

Delivering services to customers via the Internet using ArcIMS® or ArcWeb℠ Services helps to rebuild the link between people and government or between organizations and the customers they serve. It also enables organizations to meet the challenges of reducing costs, delivering services faster, providing better customer service, and increasing productivity.

GIS has a positive ripple effect

While many organizations have implemented GIS in focused projects, they can derive maximum benefits by implementing an enterprise-wide GIS program that makes GIS an integral component of their daily business work flow. Businesses have realized that success rates are increased and sustained by developing a solid foundation of data and services to apply across an entire organization to solve an array of problems. With a solid footing, a GIS can build on itself, and benefits will spill over from department to department.

Many of the case studies covered in this book show how GIS technology has become ingrained into a group's daily activities and how hard it is to imagine conducting business without GIS. A crime analyst is not only concerned with how much faster she can solve a crime with GIS, but also that the overall crime rate has gone down. GIS is a vital tool for emergency managers because of the number of lives it helps save and for its capacity to supply critical information instantly. It also enables them to study what happened during an emergency and model "what-if" scenarios, which aids in emergency planning and preparedness. Businesses use GIS to help them increase revenue and because it helps them make their business processes more efficient.

As you read these pages, you are encouraged to visualize how GIS is benefiting or could benefit your organization and those you serve. The case studies featured show how investing in GIS, while providing a common language for discussion, is a commercially sound strategy that brings stakeholders together in the decision-making process.

SAVE MONEY/ COST AVOIDANCE

The survival and success of an organization depends on many variables as management strives to become as efficient and productive as possible, maintain revenue streams, and control expenses. When income slows in a soft economy, management must move quickly to control expenditures and find ways to save money or avoid costs. Executives often turn to technology to help streamline or automate their operations, and GIS has emerged as a technology with a reputation for cutting costs related to work flows or business problems.

GIS helps control spending through direct cost savings and cost avoidance. GIS applications that improve decision making or increase productivity result in direct cost savings. GIS avoids costs when it offers efficient alternatives to meet a goal or reduces labor costs. Because GIS saves time, overtime costs can be reduced or eliminated.

Organizations use GIS to avoid costs in any number of ways. In real estate, GIS can help select the best locations to reach the most customers or serve the most citizens. A spatial analysis can guide decisions to select a less expensive property that reaches the most clients while avoiding costs. It can also predict lower travel costs or determine that fewer fleet vehicles are needed—another savings.

Responding to public inquiries is faster and easier with GIS-based Internet and intranet applications. Organizations can convert Web site visits to a work-hour equivalent, replicating staff time without adding personnel. These Web-based applications are proven alternatives to programs previously done with direct mailings, paper materials production, extended hours of operation, or the addition of locations to meet demand. GIS lets organizations do more with the same or even less money.

E-Government for planning and environmental policy issues

SECTOR *Planning*
INDUSTRY *Government*

Carl Zulick
ePlanning project manager
U.S. Department of Interior, Bureau of Land Management
Planning, Assessment, and Community Support
www.ak.blm.gov/nwnpra

The E-Government Act of 2002 calls on federal agencies to expand the use of the Internet and computer resources for delivering government services in a citizen-centered, results-oriented, and market-based environment. In response, the Bureau of Land Management (BLM), an agency within the U.S. Department of the Interior, has begun its ePlanning initiative. BLM administers 261 million surface acres of America's public lands and sustains the health, diversity, and productivity of the land for the use and enjoyment of present and future generations.

By bringing land-use planning and NEPA into the digital medium and fostering a government-to-government and government-to-citizen data and services interchange, ePlanning fulfills a critical component of the E-Government initiative.

The BLM uses information technology, especially the World Wide Web, to develop more efficient land-use planning practices and encourage an open and collaborative process. To that end, the agency launched the E-Gov for Planning and the National Environmental Policy Act of 1969 (NEPA) project. In partnership with ESRI, BLM completed a pilot project in 2003 that built a common planning data model and core land-management tools for the BLM enterprise. The project is managed from the BLM's planning, assessment, and community support group in Washington, D.C., and the BLM National Science and Technology Center in Denver.

E-Government, or ePlanning, is a project initiative that focuses on the delivery of planning information with fully integrated text, intelligent and interactive maps, and map layers. With ePlanning Web tools, planning teams can easily create integrated documents for BLM's land-use planning business. Goals of the project are to provide a common look, feel, and functionality for BLM planning and NEPA documents; a new and efficient method for public participation and collaboration in the planning process; a consistent technology implementation throughout BLM; common and reproducible work-flow processes; reusable data for processing post-planning actions; and the transition from individual land-use planning projects to a cyclical process. The ePlanning initiative establishes a new mechanism for land-use planning that supports participation, collaboration, and community-based land-use planning.

The ePlanning system is built using ArcIMS and ArcSDE® software. The system's toolbox provides users with Web-based documents enabling them to read land-use plans, submit comments, and view maps related to these plans. Interactive Web documents from ePlanning link specific sections of a land-use plan to specific geographic features on the Web-based maps. Users can click on map features to view relevant land-use plan text, identify specific land-use plan documents, and connect to locations on the landscape where land-use plan text is relevant. Public ePlanning users can submit online comments about planning documents and spatial data. Geography is central to planning, and ePlanning makes geographic data available to anyone with a computer and an Internet connection.

The project's long-term goal is to extend the one-stop portal concept to other federal agencies. By bringing land-use planning and NEPA into the digital medium and fostering a government-to-government and government-to-citizen data and services interchange, ePlanning fulfills a critical component of the E-Government initiative.

Public ePlanning also seeks to increase Internet use for building and publishing NEPA and planning documents and collaborating with constituents. It will also increase partnerships with other land-management agencies, modernize data management to support interactive digital publication while maintaining traditional paper output, and treat geospatial and attribute data as an asset and not as an expense. Finally, ePlanning will support impacted activities such as permitting, lease sales, and activity-level planning. ➢

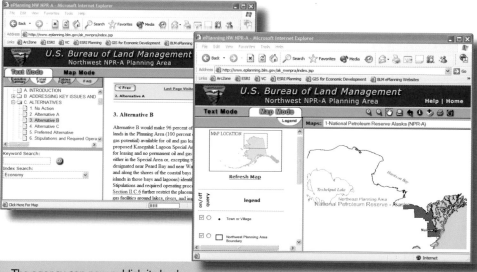

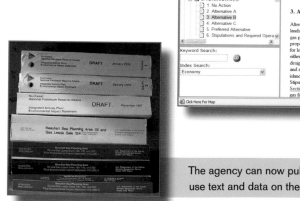

The agency can now publish its land-use text and data on the Web to avoid costly printing charges.

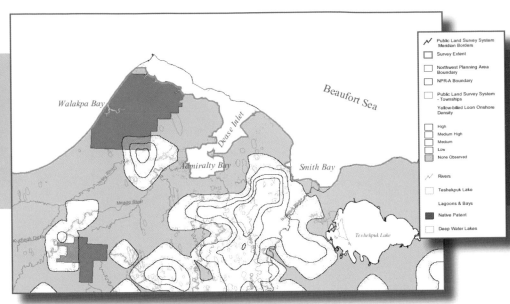

Publishing planning documents in digital form gives state, county, and community governments access to federal strategic plans.

Users of ePlanning

Intended users of this system include the public and internal bureau staff. Within BLM, users include staff at the field office, state office, and Washington, D.C. office. Land-use planning is an interdisciplinary process. Planning team leaders, writers, editors, authors, and GIS specialists will use ePlanning most intensively. Contractors hired to develop BLM land-use plans and NEPA analyses and cooperating agencies will have full access to ePlanning tools.

Estimating the number of concurrent users relies on the assumption that at full enterprise implementation, the 150 field offices that develop approximately 162 land-use plans over the ten-year planning initiative (2000–2010) will be using ePlanning. During peak plan development, an estimated three hundred BLM employees and one hundred contractors and cooperating agency employees will be using the system simultaneously. As many as five thousand people will use ePlanning within BLM. Based on the average number of hits per day to the pilot site, approximately six hundred concurrent external users will use the system to view, manipulate, and comment on land-use planning data.

Initial results, lessons learned

In the past, land-use planning teams produced many output maps that were printed in several planning documents and presented in public meetings. It took several steps to generate the correct output. In the digital realm of ePlanning, these techniques along with the GIS data are readily available to anyone with Internet access.

Users of ePlanning address the very difficult and time-consuming effort of handling scores of inquiries, comments, and protests on individual plans and will ease the burden of local and headquarters staff. Government needs to prepare NEPA documents, planning documents, and geospatial data in digital format. Other agencies and the administration are showing an increasing interest in using ePlanning tools.

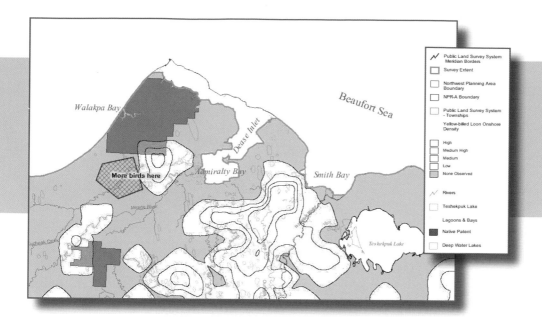

The system serves as a community outreach tool not only for federal government representatives, but also for state, county, and community governments; industries; nonprofit organizations; associations; and individuals. This is important because current E-Gov trends show that there will be more demand for online government services, resulting in a demand for more involvement in decision making, information, and coordinated and seamless government services.

Publishing land-use planning text and data on the Web will increase the accountability of the land-use planning process. Assumptions made during the process will be documented and stored in a database that can be archived in a living interactive Web-based administrative record. Tools to make the business of land-use planning more efficient, collaborative, and citizen-centered via a Web-based medium will help the BLM achieve its strategic plan goals.

Reduce costs, improve efficiencies

Because of the lack of standards throughout the bureau and the decentralized nature of state and field offices within BLM, each one of the 150 land-use planning teams develops separate formats for its land-use planning documents. Tasks pertinent to the current business process of creating the land-use plan are manual, time-consuming, data intensive, and involve numerous stages of data input.   ➢

During peak plan development, an estimated three hundred BLM employees and one hundred contractors and cooperating agency employees will be using the system simultaneously.

A planning document is created many ways. Most planning projects use a form of word processing, and some may even place the document on a shared drive for access. Delays inevitably occur when only one person at a time can access and edit the document. In instances where several individuals write multiple sections, one person is responsible for merging those sections together; managing and controlling multiple versions; and then printing, copying, and manually distributing the merged document for review. The high cost of printing limits the number of color printed maps, where they are printed, the size of the maps, and the kinds of patterns used.

"...processing a paper form costs a government $5, but generating that same form electronically costs $1.65 because it requires no labor, postage, paper, or equipment." —Planning September 2002

The receipt, recording, and categorizing of comments are currently manual processes in nearly every planning effort. There have been several attempts to semi-automate these processes because large-scale planning efforts often generate a lot of work. The ability to tie specific comments to spatial information within the planning area has never been automated and is often quite arbitrary.

According to the IBM® Institute for Electronic Government, in the article "E-Government: the Top 10 Technologies," (*Planning* September 2002), processing a paper form costs a government $5, but generating that same form electronically costs $1.65 because it requires no labor, postage, paper, or equipment. The trend is to also store planning documents electronically. ("Connected at Last in CoolTown," *Planning* July 2003) This means that cost avoidance is a significant benefit under ePlanning.

Eliminating time-consuming and costly processes

With a minimum amount of paperwork, ePlanning facilitates an openly participative, interactive land-use planning methodology. All data is placed into a relational database management system, resulting in further standardization and automation throughout the bureau.

The ePlanning project takes the existing business process and brings it into a Web medium, saving time and money. The records are automatically converted into the desired format without having to do extensive data conversion. Plan maintenance and evaluation are made easier, and public-land stakeholders find it easier to participate meaningfully in the planning process. This ultimately creates more transparency and accountability for BLM's decision-making process in land-use planning.

When implemented across the enterprise, ePlanning will result in additional cost avoidance, as field offices will not have to pay contractors for certain planning tasks such as recording, sorting, and categorizing public comments; maintaining administrative records; printing documents; and creating Web sites. The tools will be developed one time rather than more than 150 times and then installed at the bureau's twelve field offices. The high cost of printing color maps will no longer be a concern when maps are displayed on the Internet or on CD–ROM. Federal Geographic Data Committee standards and guidelines in the collection and display of metadata will be enforced and applied more consistently as data enters the ePlanning digital environment. Using the Web will enable all BLM employees to access the data they need to perform their jobs. The sharing of spatial data with the public will foster a better BLM image and increase customer and

stakeholders' efficiencies while reviewing and commenting on resource management plan documents.

Because ePlanning covers a range of resources, BLM uses information about features or activities on the earth's surface as the basis for most of its decision making. GIS technology is critical to accomplishing BLM's mission and strategic objectives. Current estimates show that approximately 90 percent of the bureau's business processes could benefit from the application of GIS. ⊙

ADDITIONAL BENEFITS

Credit union maintains fiscal stability

SECTOR *Banking and insurance*
INDUSTRY *Business*

Manju Book
GIS Manager, Arrowhead Credit Union
www.arrowheadcu.org

Arrowhead Credit Union (ACU), a medium-sized company established in 1949, is making GIS an integral component of its business work flow. Based in San Bernardino, California, with assets of $720 million, ACU uses ESRI software to improve its financial stability.

The credit union's strategic planning, marketing, and market research divisions use GIS to expand their direct marketing capabilities. It uses ArcView Business Analyst to refine direct mail strategies and target specific households to attract new members. Previously, ACU sent mailings based on ZIP Code level data with predetermined criteria from an outside source. ACU's marketing group found these methods expensive and lacked precision to attract and capture new profitable account holders. With GIS, ACU now sends specific offerings to smaller groups of households with an appropriate offering based on profiles of consumers from those areas. ACU

identifies areas of high opportunity based on profiles and other specific criteria such as drive time distance to a nearby ACU branch. GIS offers increased return on investment by decreasing the overall cost of a marketing campaign while increasing the effectiveness of each promotion.

Another division of ACU, Credit Union Services Operations, uses GIS to assist other credit unions in its league. The division offers GIS business services to assist other growing credit unions with market analysis, direct marketing, and siting. These partnerships enable a growing credit union to benefit from GIS even though it may not have the immediate budgeting available to implement a GIS. ACU uses its GIS to show these partnering credit unions where local businesses are located to target prospective employer groups that might need its services. GIS makes the credit unions aware of specific market conditions and increases their understanding about how to attract more members. This "GIS for business knowledge sharing" helps each credit union grow.

GIS helps credit unions make decisions about where to place branches and automated teller machines based on customer transactional data, deposit information, and specific data sets.

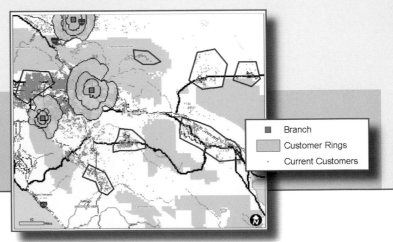

The map on the right shows selected customers (light blue) who meet the criteria for a marketing campaign (green polygons).

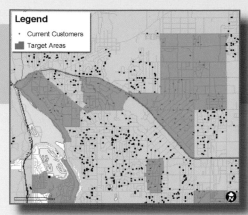

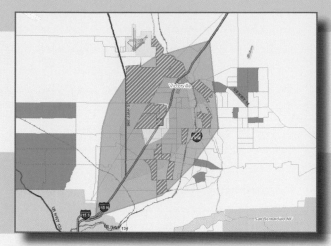

Green polygons represent areas that meet target-marketing criteria. Shaded targes are within a fifteen-minute drive time of the branch.

In addition, GIS facilitates the financial decision-making process. Knowing exactly where to place branches and automated teller machines (ATMs) is arguably the most important corporate decision a credit union will ever make. ACU's Branch Strategies group uses ArcView Business Analyst to determine the best locations for ATMs and branches based on customer transactional data, deposit information, and other specific data sets. GIS continually re-evaluates each branch and ATM location as market conditions change. The credit union once made these decisions by driving to the location or by relying on third-party data, which might be unreliable. GIS also determines which Stater Brothers supermarket will host the next in-store credit union ATM.

"An added benefit is that GIS maps also assist greatly with communications among board members," said Manju Book, ACU's GIS administrator. ⊙

"The benefits we receive far outweigh the time, cost, and effort that go into using Business Analyst."

Manju Book

Killing costs and mosquitoes

SECTOR *Health and human services*
INDUSTRY *Government*

Patrick J. Bresnahan, PhD
Geographic Information Officer, Richland County, South
Carolina
www.richlandmaps.com

At the beginning of the West Nile virus outbreak in New York, Richland County, South Carolina, decided to modernize its Vector Control Department with new technology including GIS. Vector Control was stuck in the era of paper maps, colored pencils, and a lot of redundant paperwork. It had a long way to go and a bundle of time to save.

After studying the department's needs, Richland County GIS added new computers, handheld personal digital assistants (PDAs), an Internet application, and ESRI's ArcView® and ArcPad® software. Vector Control staff was hesitant but excited about the new technology and amazed at how much time it could save.

Richland County's new mosquito control program automates Vector Control employees' work flow and business process. With GIS, Vector Control can concentrate spraying efforts on areas based on maps that visualize rainfall and mosquito counts. Vector Control employees search county GIS data for mosquito breeding sites, treat them with the proper chemical, and log activities on a PDA. At the office, employees synchronize data into a spatially enabled database for visualization in the GIS.

A department of redundancy

Before implementation of this GIS program, Vector Control employees filled out numerous paper forms in the field and then hand copied them to another sheet at the office for someone else to input into a database. This increased the risk of data error, which often went uncorrected. It was also labor intensive. Staff could not visualize spatial trends in its data and spent much of its time doing paperwork rather than killing mosquitoes.

Today, Vector Control employees enter data into their PDAs in the field. Paper forms have been

Vector control uses customized maps
that feature selected layers.

reproduced onto the PDA, thereby reducing erroneous entries. With ArcPad on their PDAs, staff can view and query the data in the field. When employees return to the office, they place their PDA into a cradle and synchronize all information into the master database. The database joins to a shapefile in ArcView for visualization. This new work flow enables the department to spend twelve to fifteen extra work-hours per week finding and killing harmful mosquitoes and other vectors, rather than filling out paperwork.

Vector Control also saves time and increases efficiency with Richland County's Internet Mapping Service Web site. Previously, employees had to make weekly trips to the Richland County assessor's office to locate complaints based in Richland County Vector Control's jurisdiction. Vector Control employees now use Richland County's publicly available mapping Web site to determine locations. This saves three to four work-hours per week.

GIS saves Richland County Vector Control an average of twenty hours per week. Assuming an average pay rate of $15 per hour, the department saves between $225 and $375 per week—a $19,500 per year savings. The Richland County GIS

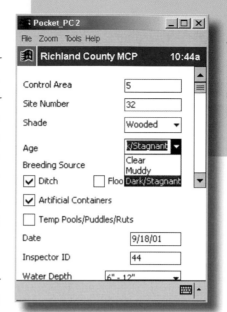

Vector control tracks field data digitally with custom iPAQ™ software.

department spent approximately $25,000 purchasing hardware and software to develop this program. Since its inception, the program has more than paid its way in increased productivity and less money spent on unnecessary paperwork. Vector Control provides a more efficient service to the taxpayers of Richland County with the help of GIS. ⊙

Richland County GIS Vector Control
15–25 hours per work savings over paperwork-based system
15–25 hours × $15 per hour = $225–$375 per week
$225–$375 × 52 weeks per year = $11,700–$19,500

Using GPS devices, all known breeding sites, monitoring sites, stations, and at-risk sites were recorded and added to the ArcView project. This allowed the human–mosquito interaction to be tracked and analyzed for trends.

ADDITIONAL BENEFITS

Playing the technology card in cost avoidance

SECTOR *Planning*
INDUSTRY *Government*

William "Pat" Egetter
Transportation and Land Management Agency
County of Riverside, California
www.tlma.co.riverside.ca.us

Riverside County is the fourth largest county in the state of California, stretching nearly 200 miles across and comprising approximately 7,300 square miles of fertile river valleys, low deserts, mountains, foothills, and rolling plains. The terrain consists of areas below sea level (the Salton Sea area in the desert) to mountains rising 10,800 feet in elevation. Riverside County shares borders with densely populated Los Angeles, Imperial, Orange, San Diego, and San Bernardino counties and extends from within 14 miles of the Pacific Ocean to the Colorado River. Riverside County is home to more than 1.6 million residents and continues to experience major growth while facing tough economic times.

During the 1980s, the county started using GIS to respond to the pressures of the phenomenal growth. During a one-year period, the county added fifty thousand new parcels and incorporated three new cities. Riverside County evolved its GIS into a multidepartment GIS to cut costs, save time, and generate revenue. The results have enabled the county to save time and money at the organization level, and county residents have realized savings.

County of Riverside Geo-Info application

Geo-Info is an ArcInfo® software-based application that uses ARC Macro Language (AML™) and a variety of programs under the more traditional UNIX® ArcInfo environment. The county started developing Parcel-Info in 1990, and since then the application has evolved into Geo-Info. Under continuous update and modification since its original development, the county's Transportation and Land Management Agency (TLMA) considers Geo-Info

"The County of Riverside is one of the nation's fastest growing regions, yet the uncertainties of the State of California's financial situation will challenge county departments' ability to deliver services. Technology will continue to play a key role in enhancing county services and keeping operations running in a cost-efficient manner. Over the years, technology has been the means of keeping staffing levels down, yet providing timely and professional quality services to the constituents in Riverside County." —Riverside County Web site

a critical application to serve the public, developers, consultants, and engineers.

Geo-Info reports can be based on one parcel, a parcel address, multiple parcels via a list, or through a pan-and-zoom method to select a particular parcel. The latter method is popular at the public information counters helping the public locate a parcel on a particular street even if the assessor's parcel number is not known.

The GIS staff supports an ongoing requirement to develop and create the full report for the end user at the public information counter within a two-minute period. This requirement has resulted in specific and streamlined applications to access parcel information that meet the business needs of the agency.

Users can review reports on screen or send them to one of many printers in various locations. Because the county covers a large area, TLMA operates full-service offices in three locations. With one location more than ninety miles away from the county seat, staff members at the remote locations use the Geo-Info application via a wide area network to serve the public.

Geo-Info's online selectable and dynamic maps enable counter land-use technicians to work with citizens to describe the opportunities and constraints for a particular parcel under consideration for development. At the counters, online map displays include nearly fifty different available data layers.

Cost-avoidance calculations for Geo-Info

Riverside County adjusted its methodology to calculate cost savings in the land development process by including full recovery cost rates for staff. These rates include salary, benefits, and department and county overhead factors when used with the development deposit-based fee programs. The county requires a deposit of funds for all development-related projects and tracks actual time worked on each project with a complex and comprehensive accounting system. This sometimes requires developers to provide more funds to the county to complete the review and processing of the project while other property owners and developers receive refunds after the project is completed. ➢

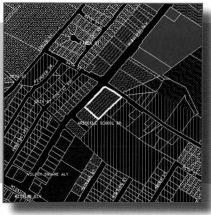

Some of the Web-based ArcInfo applications have been converted to ArcIMS, and new ArcIMS services have been developed. The Supervisorial District Viewer provides the end user with the ability to view detailed areas of a district.

Geo-Info application		
48,000 accesses (6 months) × 2	= 96,000 accesses per year	
96,000 × 40 minutes/60	= 64,000 hours of staff time	The forty minutes are based on the average amount of time it took staff to manually research information for the public information counter before implementation of this application.
64,000 × $63.00	= $4,032,000 cost avoidance per year in staff costs	The hourly productive rate for the planning aide for FY2002–2003 is $63.00/hour. This rate is used conservatively for these calculations. Actual productive rates range from $48.00/hour for land-use technicians to $115.00/hour for planning department staff.

NOTE: This number does not include the following cost savings that cannot be quantified.

1 Reduction in costs corresponding to county staff incurred by the customer for not having to wait or time required to visit the Riverside County offices.

2 Additional costs that would have been needed to add office space and staff to handle the increase in activity or visits to the public information counters. The county administrative center in the city of Riverside currently serves an average of 190 customers per day.

3 Additional time that would be necessary to research more information with manual methods. During the fourteen-year period this application has been operating, approximately forty-five additional GIS layers have been added.

4 Consistent and concise information delivered at all public information counters to the engineers, developers, consultants, and the public.

5 These calculations represent only those made by TLMA and its departments. Other county departments such as the assessor/tax collector use the application for information purposes.

6 Additional capabilities in displaying images and orthophotos within the application. Early versions of the assessor's map pages were researched by finding the map within a set of manual map books. A recent version of the application provided the capability to access and display those maps on the screen from a library of more 22,697 images.

The calculations for the cost avoidance of this application are upgraded each year. The most recent numbers were developed on January 7, 2003.

To evaluate how to develop this calculation, the county determined the average time needed to research manual maps and other information required to initiate a development application or building permit. Technicians at the counter spent an average of forty minutes assembling the information needed to process a development application or building permit.

The application reports information quickly to keep the wait to two minutes or less. TLMA did not try to quantify the cost of maintaining the various GIS layers as part of the cost avoidance because they are also used, developed, or supported by other functions of the GIS and departments using the multi-department system.

The agency considers the GIS Geo-Info application a critical application. Staff is determining how to port the application while maintaining functionality and speed to an ArcIMS and ArcSDE environment. After addressing security and privacy concerns, the county intends to develop an online public information counter that is accessible via the Internet.

GIS ArcInfo Web applications

In 1997, TLMA launched a Web site that included information for developers, engineers, and consultants and published maps with specific information on development projects. The site was developed with ArcInfo and HTML. A .gif image map file serves as the overall index. A series of .gif images enables users to view specific details within these predefined areas. An example is the environmental hazards map, which users commonly access for land development applications.

Cost-avoidance calculations for ArcInfo Web applications

These GIS query statistics are based on data from calendar year 2002 and were processed on January 9, 2003. These cost-avoidance calculations do not include figures for the county's newer ArcIMS applications.

This set of calculations was more difficult to develop because the impact on the planning department had to be estimated. There were no solid figures for the number of questions answered each month concerning zoning of a parcel. A conservative approach identified 10 percent based on discussions with various planning staff and some developers and engineers who used the Web-based services. Many other side benefits that are not included in the calculations resulted from the automation of customer requests through the Web site. These included reduced wait time for constituents processing actual permits or cases and less space required to process and handle additional customers at public counter areas. These and similar cost savings derived from Geo-Info could not be quantified.

Riverside County plans to transition its GIS from a multidepartment supported operation to a countywide enterprise GIS and to expand its Web services with GIS applications specific to the needs of each department. ☉

Transportation and Land Management Agency GIS Web applications		
Total number of hits for GIS information: 44,900 hits per month		
Total yearly hits for GIS queries: 44,900/month × 12: 538,800 hits per year		
Assumptions: An estimate of only 10 percent of these hits would have actually resulted in an individual taking the time to ask the question of agency staff either at the front counter, by phone, or by discussing the question out in the field with a planner. It is estimated that an answer takes five minutes of staff time (.0833 hrs).		
538,800 × .10	= 53,880 staff questions	The hourly rate of $63/hour is the productive hourly rate for a planning aide. However, potential staff members who typically answer public questions range from a land-use technician ($48/hour) to a planner ($115/hour).
53,880 × .0833	= 4,488 work-hours of public information	
4,488 × $63.00	= $282,744 per year cost avoidance in staff costs	

ADDITIONAL BENEFITS

Delivering accurate information on the fly and saving money

SECTOR *Economic development*
INDUSTRY *Government*

Patrick J. Bresnahan, PhD
Geographic Information Officer, Richland County, South Carolina
www.richlandmaps.com

At the close of business one day in early November 2000, T. Cary McSwain, the administrator of Richland County, South Carolina, called Patrick Bresnahan, the county's geographic information officer, for assistance with an ongoing economic development project, nicknamed Spider. A technology company evaluating land in Richland County to construct a billion dollar production facility had narrowed its search to two locations in the Southeast. Corporate representatives and their consulting engineers asked the county to pay $140,000 for a field survey of the property to assess the elevation, slope, and drainage characteristics. The survey results were to help determine costs for development of the 150-acre site. The technology firm emphasized that they needed this preliminary work completed within forty-five days to make the final site selection before the end of the calendar year.

In October, Richland County had accepted delivery of remotely sensed light detection and ranging (LIDAR) data from a mission flown during the spring of 2000. McSwain asked if the county could use the new data to satisfy the request without spending money from the general fund for preliminary site evaluations. He wanted to answer the request for financial support the following morning in a meeting with the consulting engineering firm.

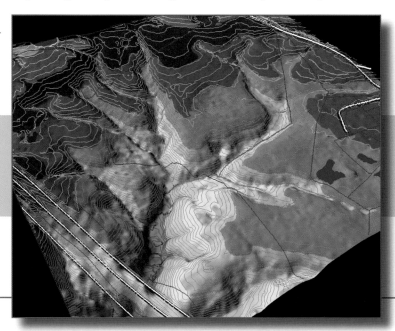

Richland County used LIDAR data to create a digital terrain model for a 150-acre site under consideration for development.

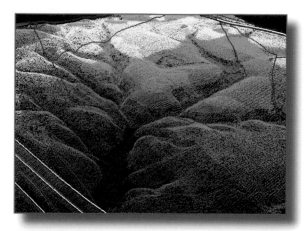

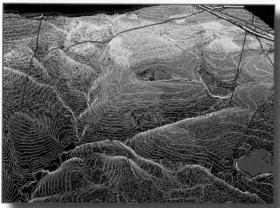

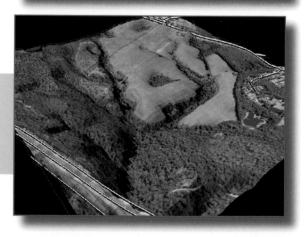

The remote sensing data and GIS saved Richland County from spending $140,000.

That evening ASCII files from the LIDAR helped create a digital terrain model (DTM) for the project area. The rough DTM of the site contained more than fifty thousand x, y, and z points. Slope, aspect, shading, two-foot contours, and potential drainage were all calculated from the resulting surface model of the site. The county used aerial photos from a previous mission to provide background for the surface features. At 8:00 A.M. the next morning, Richland County GIS staff made a presentation to McSwain and the consulting engineers, and they handed over several CDs containing source elevation and derived data for the site. The request was satisfied within twenty-four hours.

In fall 2000, the economy was on the front end of a major decline in the technology sector, and Spider was to be a computer chip production facility. The interested corporation lost more than 80 percent of its stock value in the crash of the technology sector and sold the division that was to manufacture the chips to a company overseas. The site remains undeveloped. The remote sensing data and GIS saved Richland County from spending $140,000 (hard-dollar cost savings) that would have never been returned in tax revenue. Richland County had just begun development of a county GIS in 1999, and this early return on investment solidified support for continued system implementation. ⊙

New system optimizes beverage distribution

SECTOR Logistics and fleet management
INDUSTRY Transportation (International)

Chris Walz
Vice President, RouteSmart Technologies
www.routesmart.com

In early 1999, Distributor de Bebidas Jardim América, an exclusive distributor of Antárctica beverages in São Paulo, Brazil, implemented the RouteSmart Route Optimization System. The benefits are already apparent. According to the company's administrative manager Mr. Walter Fialho, in addition to prioritizing delivery routes with the system, the company has also re-organized sales routes and is seeing an average distribution service cost savings of approximately 12.5 percent.

Fialho estimates that in less than a year, the company will save $350,000 and a return on its investment in a little more than two months.

Fialho estimates that in less than a year, the company will save $350,000 and a return on its investment in a little more than two months. The company expects to reduce the number of delivery trucks from the present fleet of seventy to sixty to further reduce costs. With fifteen thousand delivery addresses in the city of São Paulo and adjacent boroughs, Distributor de Bebidas Jardim América transports thirty different Antárctica products in 150 different packaging modes—a total of fifty thousand hectoliters delivered monthly.

Intent on upgrading its transportation logistics, the company had to overcome several obstacles such as heavily trafficked areas, limitations imposed on delivery times, seasonal flooding of roads, poorly maintained public highways, and lack of security in some regions. Today with RouteSmart software from RouteSmart Technologies of Columbia, Maryland, the organization of each delivery route considers all these variables, in sharp contrast to past policy, which prioritized deliveries exclusively on sales volumes.

The integrated GIS system enabled the company to assemble and create a GIS database with all information on its exclusive region and product delivery points. It became possible to identify each area's specific features such as maximum speed limits, one-way and divided traffic streets, topography factors, and turn restrictions. The software is also fed data on completed sales, truck tonnage capacity, loading and unloading time, schedule limitations, and specific delivery information exclusive to each sales point. With this data, RouteSmart calculates the best delivery routes.

Distributor de Bebidas Jardim América also uses the system to identify sales routes. Fialho asserted that this has eliminated ten routes previously covered by company sales representatives. The system has other advantages. "With RouteSmart, the company's dependence on the driver is lessened," Fialho said. "Previously, in many cases, if the driver did not show up, the company had a problem because only he knew that particular route."

Fialho said RouteSmart has significantly improved customer service and helped define the company's merchandising policy, describing areas that need advertisements such as refrigerated trucks bearing the Antárctica logo. The company made these improvements to all of its routes in São Paulo and is in the process of doing the same in greater Grande São Paulo.

The RouteSmart system models complex, mixed-mode (driving and walking) routing problems and solves high-density residential and low-density commercial service routing problems for daily dispatch purposes and work area design.

Along with Distribuidor de Bebidas Jardim América, postal and local delivery industry companies such as the U.S. Postal Service, FedEx Home Delivery, United Parcel Service, Hellenic Post (Greece), and Standard Coffee Service use the RouteSmart system on a nationwide basis to reduce costs, evaluate pickup and delivery operations logistics, and manage operations daily. ⊙

ADDITIONAL BENEFITS

In-house business analysis helps win theater tenant

SECTOR *Real estate*
INDUSTRY *Business*

Evelyn Hartz
Tenant Leasing Specialist, Crown American Properties, LP
www.crownamerican.com

Securing tenants to fill vacancies and keep them occupied are high priorities for Crown American Properties, LP. The real estate investment trust has twenty-seven malls located in eight states with a combined gross area to lease of about sixteen million square feet. To attract retail tenants to mall leases, Crown American Properties realized it needed to offer prospective clients as much data as possible and faster than the competition. Producing detailed market information would often cost thousands of dollars and weeks of outside consultant work. Crown American Properties needed an alternative solution. Implementing ArcView Business Analyst software from ESRI, the company quickly provided its clients and prospects with accurate reports and detailed maps of many market areas, saving time and the cost of hiring outside analysts.

ArcView Business Analyst helped Crown American Properties pursue a major movie theater tenant for the West Manchester Mall in York, Pennsylvania. A client was concerned about the number of competing cinemas in the vicinity. Crown American Properties quickly identified the theaters in the surrounding areas, geocoding their addresses, and mapping them using the Store Setup wizard in ArcView Business Analyst. The map provided visual details that would be unseen in tabular data. A list of the addresses meant nothing to the prospective tenant, but the map showed all the competitors located on the east side, with none near the West Manchester Mall. Crown American Properties performed demographic analysis of the area with the GIS and presented the results in a full-color map along with a comprehensive report. The result: a signed lease agreement and a new theater in York, Pennsylvania.

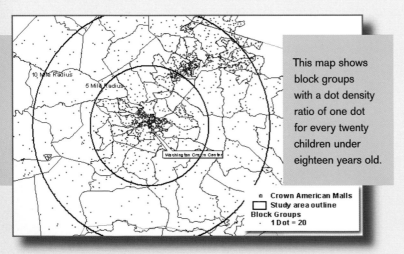

This map shows block groups with a dot density ratio of one dot for every twenty children under eighteen years old.

"The biggest selling point for us," said Evelyn Hartz, tenant-leasing specialist for Crown American, "was the bundling of the information. All of the variables were there in one place. We've noticed that when our leasing agents use a proposal packet that contains maps and reports along with charts and other regional background data, the lease-signing process seems to go much faster." ⊙

ADDITIONAL BENEFITS

SAVE TIME

Administrators and others involved in time management will find GIS a valuable tool. Besides saving work-hours and increasing turnaround time on tasks and projects, GIS benefits an organization's ability to do jobs that would otherwise be shifted to overtime, delayed, or left undone. Organizations that apply georeengineering efforts to increase efficiency or productivity can accomplish more tasks in the same period.

Time is money, and GIS bears that out as it gives organizations savings in both. GIS applications free staff time and shift workloads. Analyses with GIS range from performing multiple "what-if" scenarios to automating entire manual processes. With a GIS, tasks that took hours, weeks, or months to complete are finalized in minutes. Integrating GIS in mobile and Internet-based applications has yielded trip reductions by customers traveling to a location and employees to a job site.

GIS has proven itself as a success in time management to help businesses meet their planning goals, despite the perception that there is never enough time to move an organization forward or increase customer satisfaction.

Closing in on Hurricane Isabel

SECTOR *Public safety*
INDUSTRY *Government*

Will Aycock
GIS Coordinator, City of Wilson, North Carolina
www.wilsonnc.org

With the 2003 hurricane season looming, the city of Wilson, North Carolina, prepared for the worst with several new GIS applications in place. The preparations paid off that September as Hurricane Isabel threatened the East Coast.

City staff used the GIS for pre-incident analysis of flood-prone areas to prepare street closures, position resources, track feeder lines that lose power, identify critical-care customers served by the feeder lines without power, and monitor incidents as they unfolded. The new GIS applications assisted in the planning and response effort for Hurricane Isabel and provided information that will enable GIS to be more useful during future emergencies.

In the days leading up to the hurricane, the city conducted an analysis of historical flood events and FEMA-designated flood hazard areas. The analysis quickly revealed areas that could become isolated during major flooding. In addition, the analysis identified sections of streets that become hazardous during floods. This information gave planners time to put emergency response resources in areas that might become isolated. The city made tentative plans to block and reroute six streets prone to flooding. Fortunately, streams were running at low levels and Isabel brought relatively small amounts of precipitation. While the city escaped relatively unscathed, the analysis is notable because flooding is an issue that Wilson likely will face in future storms.

During the storm, the Emergency Operations Center (EOC) used GIS to track feeder lines as they went down and came back up. This enabled everyone in the EOC to graphically understand what portions of the service area were without power. In addition, they could search addresses to determine if they were served by an offline feeder line. The depiction of offline feeders in GIS also supplied a rough estimate of customers affected by power outages.

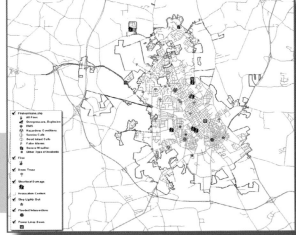

Flooded intersections, structural damage, and other hurricane-related damage around Wilson, North Carolina, were pinpointed in the emergency operations center.

Identifying those in need

As the operations center collected information on out-of-service feeder lines, it identified customers served by those lines. It also used the utility billing database and the customer point file to identify customers who were medically dependent on power. The operations center sent the information to the 911 center or to Wilson Fire/Rescue Services, which called those customers to see if they needed help.

Throughout the day of September 18, the operations center plotted all information on the GIS. Everyone there could see the plotted incidents via a projector connected to a GIS laptop. The operations center tracked data on downed power lines, downed trees, house fires, flooding, and structural damage as it came in. The map displayed blocked streets and unfolding events for everyone to see. ➤

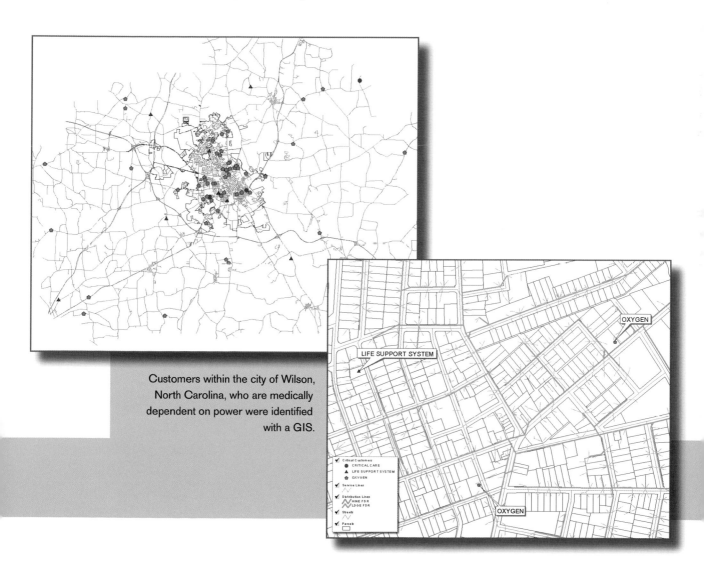

Customers within the city of Wilson, North Carolina, who are medically dependent on power were identified with a GIS.

Post-implementation analysis

The use of GIS vastly improved Wilson's response during Hurricane Isabel. Even so, the city sees room to improve. For Hurricane Isabel, the public services and fire department were the only agencies aware of the flood-prone area analysis. A review of the event found the city should share this information with police and utilities so they can move resources into threatened areas before a storm arrives. It's unlikely we will experience another flood event of the same magnitude as Hurricane Floyd, which came prior to Isabel. Nevertheless, we must prepare for such a flood.

> *The use of GIS vastly improved Wilson's response during Hurricane Isabel.*

Following customer calls in the GIS would also significantly improve tracking of power outages, rather than tracking which feeder lines are out. This would more accurately show scattered power outages. The existing methods did not identify critical-care customers who lost their service lines, and current methods sometimes missed portions of feeder lines that went down during Hurricane Isabel.

The city could identify likely trouble spots if each customer who called in a report was logged into the GIS. Furthermore, tracking every affected customer would provide a more definitive count of those customers. This manner of tracking would also quickly identify repeat calls to prevent duplicate work orders. The city could coordinate recovery efforts using data from every call logged into the GIS and support post-incident analysis of outages.

The system relies on tracking each power outage to identify customers who need power for medical reasons. This application is also dependent upon the utility billing database to identify critical-care customers. The city must communicate the need for callers to identify themselves as medically dependent. This will help ensure the city is using the most accurate and complete database possible during a storm event. The city plans to develop a standard response to critical-care patients who lose power.

Tracking incidents in an EOC currently requires communication from the field and has been a successful method of data collection. Its success could be broader if all parties involved understood the importance of communicating information to the center and the individual responsible for entering the data into the GIS. All calls to the 911 center will appear on the map once the GIS and 911 systems are linked. ⊙

Cities paint their future

In July 2003, the Northeastern Illinois Planning Commission (NIPC) completed what is believed to be the largest interactive use of GIS for regional planning in the country. NIPC is the regional planning agency for metropolitan Chicago and the surrounding six counties, comprising a total of 272 municipalities. One of NIPC's primary responsibilities is maintaining a thirty-year growth forecast that underpins regional transportation investments and other infrastructure planning. NIPC has a tradition of bottom-up, collaborative forecasting using in-person consultations in each of the affected 272 cities. These are critical sessions in which local officials and NIPC staff share development information and preferences for growth boundaries and future land-use patterns.

In the past, participants accomplished this process using manual drawings on paper maps. They converted the maps into population and employment estimates for eventual reconciliation with regional forecast totals. While solidly grounded in local collaboration, it proved cumbersome, inefficient, and prone to error, and took more than forty-five hundred hours to complete. That's when NIPC decided it needed an interactive GIS tool that could be taken to local meetings and used on the fly to capture stakeholders' spatial inputs. According to Michael K. Smith, NIPC's president, "We've been an

SECTOR *Planning*
INDUSTRY *Government*

Max Dieber
Director of Research Services,
Northeastern Illinois Planning Commission
www.nipc.cog.il.us

ESRI user for many years at the regional scale, and we knew that the technology was becoming more portable and interactive, so it was a natural choice for our process."

During the past year, "painting sessions" have been held with 210 of the region's 272 municipalities.

Called Paint the Town, NIPC's interactive tool enables users to draw growth boundaries and "paint" land uses on the fly during public meetings. As areas are painted, the tool simultaneously calculates which households and jobs are being added to a community. Painting is accomplished with a palette of land uses that offers different choices of development style and intensity. Paint the Town is a customization of the INDEX planning support system offered by Criterion Planners/Engineers of Portland, Oregon (*www.crit.com*). During the past year, "painting sessions" have been held with 210 of the region's ➤

"We've been an ESRI user for many years ... so it was a natural choice for our process."

Michael K. Smith, NIPC's president

At regional outreach meetings, the Northeastern Illinois Planning Commission staff prepared a comprehensive digital record for further analysis with local officials.

272 municipalities where local officials used a touch-sensitive screen to draw and paint their preferred growth scenarios. The objective is to give as much freedom and creativity as possible to users within the bounds of standard GIS functions and data.

At the conclusion of the outreach meetings, NIPC staff has a comprehensive digital record that can be left with local officials and analyzed further at the commission headquarters. Ultimately, individual community scenarios are aggregated into the multi-county growth forecast. "This is a great example of a relatively simple piece of technology making a world of difference in an important job for hundreds of communities," said Ron Thomas, the commission's executive director. NIPC staff completed the outreach meetings with a two-person team, one laptop running Paint the Town, and about two to three hours of time with local officials—a 46 percent time savings over the manual method. The initial round of sessions used an ArcView 3.2 version of Paint the Town to gain operating experience and enhancement ideas. These have now been used to create an ArcGIS® version for the forecasting cycle in 2005.

In evaluating lessons learned thus far, NIPC has demonstrated that a GIS-based explanation of forecast information and on-the-fly scenario creation by nontechnical local officials is not only feasible but also equally important as an engaging technique for interagency collaboration. The commission believes the process improved information gathering about local expectations and aspirations and helped build credibility for forecasts and NIPC while saving a considerable amount of time. The positive experience led forty-five communities to ask for their own copies of Paint the Town, and NIPC is expanding its use of the tool into its regional planning and local technical assistance programs. ☉

Before GIS / Paint the Town	With GIS / Paint the Town
4,500 hours needed	2,100 hours needed: a 46 percent time savings
Four staff people involved	Four staff people involved
Total hours saved: 2,400 (or approximately one person-year of labor)	

ADDITIONAL BENEFITS

Charlotte gets smart about waste collection routing

The city of Charlotte, North Carolina, has saved a significant number of work-hours by integrating GIS into its refuse collection process. Charlotte had adopted a system from RouteSmart Technologies of Columbia, Maryland, to automate its routing

SECTOR *Logistics and fleet management*
INDUSTRY *Transportation*

Chris Walz
Vice President, RouteSmart Technologies
www.routesmart.com

and replace the old-fashioned tools of wall maps, pushpins, and colored pencils. Staffers manually keyed routes into the customer service database of 150,000 addresses because the city lacked technology to interact between routing and customer service. This took a great deal of time and resulted in inaccuracies, inefficiency, and waning revenues.

The old system meant frequent overtime and equipment problems on some collection routes, while high slack times plagued other routes. To help resolve the discrepancies, the department decided to implement RouteSmart GIS.

RouteSmart automatically partitions collection routes and balances crew workloads. In configuring new routes, RouteSmart includes travel times between an office or depot and the disposal site. It can also factor in nonproductive work time as part of its calculations. RouteSmart includes the mix of vehicles used to collect trash and enables users to better manage vehicles of varying capacities, matching them with collection sites and routing them more efficiently. The algorithmically savvy software allocates vehicles to streets based on an array of mixed fleet variables and street restrictions including right-of-way restrictions.

The city saw tangible results in a year. Staff estimated that RouteSmart saved Charlotte a significant number of work-hours and provided a good base for creating routes quickly. Charlotte has since purchased an additional system for its water department. ◉

Charlotte, North Carolina, saves work-hours by automatically specifying collection routes and crew workloads with a GIS application from RouteSmart Technologies.

ADDITIONAL BENEFITS

Pioneering GIS in the Southwest

SECTOR *Planning*
INDUSTRY *Government*

Neal Weinberg
Albuquerque GIS Manager, Planning Department
City of Albuquerque, New Mexico
www.cabq.gov.gis

Albuquerque, New Mexico, marks the geographic intersection of U.S. Interstates 25, 40, and old Route 66 and is recognized as the commercial, educational, cultural, and high-tech hub of the Southwest. *Newsweek*, *U.S. News & World Report*, *Money*, and *Entrepreneur* magazines have listed Albuquerque as one of the best places to live in the United States. With an area of 187 square miles and a growing population of nearly 600,000, Albuquerque is under constant pressure to expand development and services—fire and police protection, affordable housing, utilities, and education choices.

"GIS replaced the old manual drafting methods, and we still have the same amount of staff we had seventeen years ago doing many more things we weren't able to do seventeen years ago." —Neal Weinberg

The city embraces innovation, and in January 1986, its planning department started to develop what has become a dependable GIS system. "We are a relatively low-tech office, and we provide an operations function. There may not be a lot of 'gee-whiz' stuff to write articles about, but we perform an essential and valuable service for our city government," said Neal Weinberg, GIS manager in the planning department.

In January 1986, Albuquerque became the second municipality to adopt GIS technology. Its desire to be at the leading edge of technology makes Albuquerque a pioneer in GIS applications and a creative entity in managing human, technological, and geographic resources. According to Weinberg, "GIS replaced the old manual drafting methods, and we still have the same amount of staff we had seventeen years ago doing many more things we weren't able to do seventeen years ago."

Planning department staffers know the meaning of doing more with less. The department increased its GIS capabilities and productivity while the city's population increased more than 20 percent. Working to reduce urban sprawl and develop targeted areas, the department can identify areas in the city for potential growth or infill by reviewing just two GIS data layers—land use and zoning.

Creativity, savvy, and efficiency are hallmarks of the Albuquerque GIS program. "In 1986 there was a lot of skepticism," explained Weinberg. "Bear in mind the time frame we are talking about. The planning was really going on in 1985, and there were very few other municipal GIS sites. Back then it was considered some novelty or gimmick and a very expensive one at that. We had one mayor who said, 'What do we need GIS for when we have our map

Albuquerque, New Mexico's Planning Department has found GIS to be an important tool to encourage and promote quality growth and sensible planning within the city.

atlas books?' because he didn't realize the additional functionality available."

GIS encourages and promotes quality growth. If a developer needs to know spatial elements, such as lot size or development or zoning status, the planning department can quickly find the data using GIS. In the past this would have required contacting real estate agents, searching zone atlases to determine zoning (e.g., residential or manufacturing), and then cross-referencing that data with other information to learn if the land was developed. The process time has been cut from weeks to minutes. Other relevant data such as water and sewer availability can also be found because of information sharing with other city departments.

The planning department can quickly answer questions and gather needed information from this database. "I am often contacted by people who are looking for information, and they need it really fast," Weinberg said. "We can retrieve that information whether it's a complex or simple query such as the size of a building or the value of a parcel of land. People who come to us with a desperate need for accurate information are rarely disappointed."

Today, GIS has spread through most city departments. In addition to doing custom mapping and analysis, one of the primary roles of the Albuquerque GIS is gathering data that is used by all departments. The city now performs applications in record time and in an efficient manner. ⊙

20 YEARS AGO: manual process (without GIS)	TODAY: with enterprise GIS
Process: Check color map on the wall Check aerial photography Look up zone atlas (Note: data may have been outdated and was in hard copy) Data cannot be combined (overlaid) Data cannot be saved simultaneously Process would have required contacting all the real estate agents in the area or having an intern go over the zone atlas page by page and find all the manufacturing zones and cross-referencing the data with other information to find out if the land was developed or undeveloped.	Process: Query GIS systems Automatically query databases maintained by other departments (Note: digital data is up-to-date)
Duration: up to three weeks	Duration: only minutes
A single project can tie up staff for up to a month	GIS staff available to work on other infill queries or any other GIS application

ADDITIONAL BENEFITS

INCREASE EFFICIENCY

GIS is an invaluable tool for increasing productivity without waste in business operations. When businesses increase efficiency, they realize improvements in the delivery, enhancement, and more effective use of a service. Many organizations periodically rethink and reengineer their business work flows to improve the effectiveness of processes and advance their overall mission. These efforts usually result in improved service delivery by eliminating redundant or outdated steps in old processes, finding ways to alter or reduce staff workloads and trips, and developing new and innovative procedures. GIS reengineering or georeengineering requires management to look at the role geography plays in its business processes or how geography can act as an interface to deliver a service.

A common GIS reengineering or georeengineering application involves the movement of employees in the field, which generally means routing workers within specified time constraints. Another frequent business problem is how to give employees access to a knowledge base from which they can retrieve information in the course of answering customer inquiries or making other business decisions. GIS can help resolve or alleviate these kinds of dilemmas by linking all or most business data with its geographic or location component. Transferring these concepts into GIS applications of e-government or e-business can serve as an extension of staff delivering customer service twenty-four hours a day, seven days a week.

When workers collect data in the field that is related to a specific location, the implementation of a mobile GIS will enable them to travel with geographic-related data and reduce or eliminate repeat trips back to the office for information or files. Data collected in the field is accurately entered once and uploaded into the main database for immediate use.

A good approach to considering ways to increase efficiency with GIS is to list all tasks that require reengineering and then identify their geographic components. This strategy leads to increased savings of staff time and resources while achieving greater productivity and speed.

Tribe work efficiently saves time, money, and lives while preserving a culture

SECTOR *Public safety*
INDUSTRY *Tribal government*

Frank Roberts
GIS Manager, Coeur d'Alene Tribe
www.cdatribe-nsn.gov/gis

You might not expect to stumble across high technology in a land of majestic beauty, but that's just what you'll find in northern Idaho, where the Coeur d'Alene Tribe started a GIS program in part to preserve and protect that beauty.

The Coeur d'Alene Indian Reservation encompasses approximately 345,000 acres of breathtaking mountains, forests, lakes, streams, and farmland. Its people have lived in the region for centuries and traded with other tribes throughout the Pacific Northwest, Canada, and the Great Plains. Filled with natural beauty, the area attracts many tourists, and its abundance of natural resources has attracted mining and timber operations. For more than a century, the mining and smelting businesses throughout Idaho's Silver Valley produced billions of dollars in silver, lead, and zinc, but they have taken a toll on the environment. The Silver Valley, which lies within the Coeur d'Alene's aboriginal territory, is the second largest Superfund site in the United States.

Preserving a culture

The influx of people and increased forestry and mining activities have caused a range of environmental impacts. In 1991, the Coeur d'Alene Tribe realized it needed a more effective way to manage its resources. "We used GIS as an analysis tool to assist with a large natural resource damage assessment study within the tribe's aboriginal territory," said the tribe's GIS manager, Frank Roberts, but it soon became clear that GIS could assist the tribe with other projects.

The Coeur d'Alene tribal government's GIS program started with one employee and has since expanded to eight. Their duties have ranged from helping the tribe map forestry activities, implement community development programs, and generate a land-parcel database to assist tribal efforts with fish, water, and wildlife programs, lake management, and cleanup efforts at the sites affected by the mining activity. The Coeur d'Alene Reservation currently has one of the most advanced GIS programs of any tribal government.

Roberts explained that while the tribal government deals with many of the same issues that confront federal, state, and local governments, the tribe also tracks cultural information. "We have only a handful of elders who speak the native language of the Coeur d'Alene people," said Roberts. "GIS is enabling us to document the language and map the geographic places that it speaks about. We are preserving something that might have been lost forever. For this work alone, GIS is invaluable to the tribal council, the elders, and our future generations."

Fighting fires

Currently, the Coeur d'Alene tribal GIS program works with the Bureau of Indian Affairs at the U.S. Department of the Interior, Idaho Department of Lands, St. Maries Fire District, and the Worley Fire District to compile detailed structural information for map books that will be placed in fire trucks. The ArcPad Structure Mapping Project involves using handheld integrated GIS and GPS devices to collect data on every structure within the reservation and fire districts.

From June through November 2002, two data collectors walked or drove to each structure then recorded data on a mobile computing device equipped with ArcPad. At each structure, they logged information important to firefighters, including the address, type of roof, building materials, water source and fuel tank locations, vegetation densities, distance from the main road, and topography. They also took a digital photo of the building, which is linked to the data. From ArcPad, they uploaded data from each structure to the tribe's main computer database, where it is compiled and organized for the map books.

The ArcPad Structure Mapping Project produced data for 7,981 structures. The tribe initially expected to collect data at a rate of thirty structures per day, but the actual average collection rate was seventy to eighty structures a day—more than doubling the rate and cutting collection time in half, to about one minute. ➢

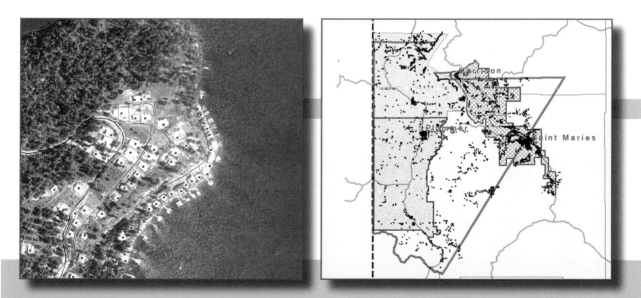

The Coeur d'Alene Tribal GIS program produced the ArcPad Structure Mapping Project, which included data for approximately eight thousand structures within the tribal district. The information is published in map books to help the fire department locate roads, hydrants, structural characteristics, and other important information.

The map books will show information about roads, hydrants, bridges, and waterways. They will also include structure characteristics, which were gathered during the first phase of the project. Photos will be available to firehouse computers where they can be printed when emergency calls come in. These books and photos will make crucial information available to firefighters before they arrive on scene.

This project could have been completed without GIS, either using blank sheets of paper or the existing parcel maps. The characteristics would have been handwritten and then entered into the database manually, a time-consuming and less accurate process than the ArcPad Structure Mapping Project.

With the help of GIS, the map books will provide another resource to improve firefighters' response time. The fire department also plans to use the books to help prevent and predict future emergencies. ⊙

ArcPad structure mapping Coeur d'Alene Tribe GIS	
Total number of structures to be mapped: 7,981 including rural and urban areas	
All structures with ArcPad	All structures without ArcPad
Mean = 40 structures per day 117 Structures = Maximum per day 7981/40 = 199 days (39.8 working weeks)	30 structures per day 7981/30 = 266 days (53.2 working weeks)

Number of days saved: 67 days, or 13.4 working weeks	
Progress made in cities (statistics from city of St. Maries)	Mean = 76 homes per day 110 homes = Maximum per day

"We have only a handful of people who speak the native language of the Coeur d'Alene people. GIS is enabling us to document the language and map the geographic places that it speaks about. We are preserving something that might have been lost forever. For this work alone, GIS is invaluable to the tribal council, the elders, and our future generations."

Frank Roberts

ADDITIONAL BENEFITS

Arkansas town implements Megan's Law

SECTOR *Public safety*
INDUSTRY *Government*

Shelby Johnson
Arkansas Geographic Information Office
www.gis.state.ar.us

In the United States, the 1994 Jacob Wetterling Act requires states to register individuals convicted of sex crimes against children. Megan's Law, signed by President Clinton in 1996, gives states the discretion to establish criteria to disclose sex offenders to the public. The process of registration and notification can take a lot of time and money, and accuracy is paramount.

The city of Fort Smith, Arkansas, has modified its sex offender notification process with a GIS. The procedure used to take forty work-hours at a cost of $460 to the city. Now, the GIS identifies addresses to be notified with its mail merge option and has reduced overall time and money expenditures by 95 percent. ⊙

Without GIS	With GIS	Saves
40 work-hours $11.54/hour = $461.60	2 work-hours $11.54/hour = $23.08	38 work-hours $11.54/hour = $438.52/week
95 percent reduction in time and money spent		

Massachusetts town efficiently manages public notifications

SECTOR Administration/Management
INDUSTRY Government

Feng Yang
GIS Manager, Town of Brookline, Massachusetts
www.town.brookline.ma.us/gis

The regulations associated with many local government proceedings might seem arcane to some, but most are rooted in the concept of serving the public. One of these rules requires public agencies to notify local citizens of proceedings that might affect them. Because assessors' offices maintain tax lists with homeowner information, they are usually tasked with providing lists of adjacent property owners and addresses.

In Brookline, Massachusetts, city hall is obliged to notify all parties of interest about hearings for zoning appeals cases, liquor or food license applications, and public works projects. Parties of interest generally include property owners and residents adjacent to the lot in question and sometimes those citizens who might be affected within a prescribed distance of the property such as a three-hundred-foot buffer.

Before Brookline implemented its GIS program, preparing lists of abutting property owners was a painstaking process, and each list could take as long as eight hours of staff time to prepare. Clerks copied pages from the assessor's map book, pasted the relevant sheets together, and drew a buffer with a compass to identify all the affected parcels. They either created a Microsoft® Word® document to produce the mailing labels or addressed the envelopes by hand. This manual procedure was not without error and often the abutters lists were inaccurate.

In 1996, Brookline started integrating GIS into its business processes. "Our original goal was to be able to update our assessor's maps as changes occurred," says Brookline GIS manager, Feng Yang. With a GIS in place, Brookline developed an application to generate the notification lists. Yang says, "Now, clerks press five buttons and they get a list of abutters, a map, and a set of predefined mailing labels. It takes them five to ten minutes to get an accurate count." This more efficient way to manage the town's information saves time and increases accuracy in notifying citizens.

The ability to share information among various departments also has been a big plus. Yang says, "Brookline's GIS system has enabled staff in the town clerk's, planning, and selectmen's office to work more efficiently, improve the quality of work, get critical information to decision makers in a timely fashion, and save time and resources by sharing information and reducing redundancy."

"The Brookline GIS is a townwide integrated system and a program that serves the public and all departments internally. It is the hub for all GIS activities throughout the town."

Feng Yang

In the seven years since it has been in use, all internal departments and the public have benefited from GIS. By using GIS-generated street maps that also identified student addresses, the transportation coordinator saved the school district hours of fieldwork. To establish drug-free school zones for the police department, the system calculated distances between crime activity, schools, and parks. This resulted in a significant savings of staff time. ⊙

To notify parties of interest about various pending cases in the planning and public works department, Brookline, Massachusetts, uses its GIS program to draw buffers and identify affected parcels.

ADDITIONAL BENEFITS

San Antonio trims inefficiencies from street-cutting permits

SECTOR *Public works*
INDUSTRY *Government*
City of San Antonio, Texas
www.maps.sanantonio.gov

San Antonio, Texas, charms visitors with its many scenic and historical attractions. While the home of the Alamo and the cobblestone River Walk has managed to preserve history and culture, it has a burgeoning urban aspect to its personality as the eighth largest city in the United States.

In the first three months, the city registered more than seventy-five hundred permits using the permit module. Staff members estimate they receive 90 percent of all permit applications online, and the number of employee hours required to approve a single permit application has decreased 71 percent from two hours to only thirty-five minutes.

San Antonio receives an estimated ninety thousand applications for street-cutting permits each year. Before contractors can commence digging in streets or rights-of-way to repair or install utilities, they must apply for a permit with the city. By early 2001, the city's permitting process within the Department of Streets was stalled. The cumbersome, paper-based process slowed permit approval, and city officials could not access critical information. The process caused backlogs, suboptimal compliance revenue, and infrastructure project conflicts and delays. The system made it difficult to coordinate work and costly to rework the same sections of roadway.

Contractors seeking a street-cutting permit had to visit the department in person and fill out an application. Applications were forwarded to the right-of-way management office where they passed through multiple levels of review. City officials estimated it took an average of two employee hours to amend, approve, or reject a single permit application.

The city did not store approved paper permits in files organized by location. The lack of a central, easily accessible repository made accessing necessary information a complex and difficult task for city staff to track and find compliance violations associated with each permit. As a result, the city would schedule two projects for the same place and time, unnecessarily recut and resurface roads, and leave traffic barricades and detours in place too long. It also left the city's compliance revenue lower than it could have been.

Rising above the paper maze

In 2001, San Antonio's Department of Streets engaged an ESRI business partner, Syncline, Inc., to work with city staff and develop a prototype permit module solution. The team deployed the MapCiti Permit Module, powered by ESRI's ArcIMS software, to manage the entire street-cutting permit process.

The system provides comprehensive, Web-enabled permitting functionality and is integrated with the city's GIS. With a standard Web browser, department staff and contractors can access and view all street, zoning, and permit activity online using maps created with the permit module. Contractors can apply for street-cutting permits and obtain automatically calculated permit fee information at any time. Staff can review and approve permit applications and track permit compliance—all online. The module helps ensure that projects do not interfere with each other and that companies comply with city guidelines. An added benefit is that city officials can develop insight into trends and patterns in street-cutting activities that were not readily apparent with the paper process.

"Syncline has given us an unprecedented ability to manage the thousands of projects going on in the city at a given time and make sure they're done in an orderly fashion," said Joe Chapa, San Antonio's GIS manager. "[The MapCiti Permit Module] has enabled us to simplify our invoicing procedure so we are more effective at applying and billing compliance fees."

In the first three months, the city registered more than seventy-five hundred permits using the permit module. Staff members estimate they receive 90 percent of all permit applications online, and the number of employee hours required to approve a single permit application has decreased 71 percent from two hours to only thirty-five minutes.

"By putting this entire function on the Web, we save time and energy, both for ourselves and for the companies that work on the city's infrastructure," said Chapa. ⊙

ADDITIONAL BENEFITS

Energy giant uses GIS to streamline meter rereads

SECTOR *Electric and gas*
INDUSTRY *Utilities*

CenterPoint Energy
www.centerpointenergy.com

CenterPoint Energy is one of the largest electricity and natural gas delivery companies in the United States. Its gas and electric meter rereads had been handled separately after two different billing systems rejected them. The ArcLogistics™ Route application now provides CenterPoint Energy with an efficient means of routing meter rereads. The software merges both lists of meter rereads daily, providing Houston-based CenterPoint Energy with an annual savings of $40,000 in reduced overtime and fleet costs. ESRI's ArcLogistics Route software solved the utility's complex routing and scheduling problems. ⊙

ADDITIONAL BENEFITS

Team effort saves a bundle for Sumter, South Carolina

Set in the heart of South Carolina, historic Sumter and Sumter County are growing communities that lead the state in per capita job growth. The city and county share a lot more than just a name. The relationship between the two serves as a model throughout South Carolina for how cooperation can reduce inefficiency.

SECTOR *Planning*
INDUSTRY *Government*

Keith Cooke
Local Government Manager
Geographic Information Services, Inc.
www.gis-services.com

At the Sumter City–County Planning Commission, GIS is a shining example of how this kind of collaboration brings about greater efficiency. Along with guiding the area's growth and ensuring a strong community character, the planning commission has many day-to-day responsibilities, including ruling on rezoning petitions filed by the public and tracking land-use cases. The planning commission had used a labor-intensive, manual, paper-based filing system to monitor these cases.

A team effort among the planning commission, the city–county GIS department, ESRI, and G/I/S produced a GIS solution that reduced the time spent monitoring these cases by 90 percent. The planning commission saved the equivalent of two months of personnel time during the first year of the new system.

> *A team effort … produced a GIS solution that reduced the time spent monitoring these cases by 90 percent.*

The application, which uses ArcView and Zoning Analyst, streamlines work flows and provides a spatial reference for each case. Zoning Analyst tracks land-use cases, creates parcel buffers, and generates public notification letters. The system enables more efficient internal operations and supplies the public with timely information.

The planning commission has found new uses for the software including an inspection of the National Flood Insurance Program. The GIS Department identified and documented twenty-three hundred properties in the flood zone in less than a day—a process that previously took up to eight weeks. This new project should upgrade the county's rating in the Federal Emergency Management Agency's community rating system by one level, which would save the public up to 4 percent on its flood insurance premiums. ⊙

ADDITIONAL BENEFITS

INCREASE ACCURACY

People need accurate information to make informed decisions. In fact, most projects begin with identifying the best and most reliable information sources.

Often the GIS combines information sources that provide the most accurate, up-to-date facts to the most departments or individuals. The basemaps used to build the foundation of the GIS are generally derived from surveying or engineering drawings. The system will cleanse or verify the accuracy of information by searching the database and isolating questionable data inputs. Several different departments might input address data as a key field; by cross-referencing these data sources and defining data standards to create a more accurate database, the GIS delivers a more accurate result. Moreover, the integration of precision support technologies, such as GPS, orthophotography, remote sensing, geopositioned video, and satellite imagery, increases the validity of GIS databases.

Accurate information contributes to the improvement of an organization's effectiveness and benefits many departments within a business or agency. In planning or public works departments, an accurate GIS could affect a decision to include or exclude a group from a program or fee structure. For instance, the number of homeowners who purchase additional insurance to comply with revised flood insurance rate maps could change dramatically when the GIS combines multiple databases for enhanced accuracy.

Accuracy also helps improve efficient and productive performance. While GIS is a technology and science designed to apply geographic analyses and reporting to the world's problems, the results of these functions are highly dependent on accurate spatial and tabular data sources. GIS increases accuracy, and that results in better decisions, analyses, reports, routing solutions, and other products.

Appreciating accuracy at American Electric Power

SECTOR *Electric and gas*
INDUSTRY *Utilities*

Paige Medlin
UCLID Software, LLC
www.uclid.com

Serving nearly five million customers, American Electric Power (AEP) is the largest electricity utility and generator in the United States, with a generating capacity of more than forty-two thousand megawatts. Originally incorporated in New York as American Gas and Electric Company in 1906, the company has a long history of innovation. In addition to building the first long-distance transmission line and the first "super" power plant in 1917, AEP consistently builds some of the most efficient generating stations in America. In 1983, AEP moved its headquarters to Columbus, Ohio.

[Williams] works an estimated 50- to 75-percent faster when he uses IcoMap on scanned deeds than if he keyed in the calls.

Like any company that has operated for nearly a century, AEP has a massive accumulation of records. Decades of acquisitions make managing this information even more complex. The utility's land records, dating nearly 150 years, are decentralized. The documents were stored in file cabinets at various offices, many in Virginia and Michigan. Most of the records are either deeds or hand-drawn maps. Although the company manages approximately 300,000 acres of land in fourteen states, there was no way to see this information in one map.

To remedy the situation, AEP is building a GIS to manage property information. Property plays a key role in its operations because it uses land for power plants, oil and gas leases, mineral rights, and forestry. AEP generates revenue by the way it uses land, and sometimes it is more profitable to sell the land.

The property must be accurately mapped before any sale. Maps help real estate agents, and potential buyers often require maps. In addition, AEP's legal department uses maps as a legal instrument. Mike Williams oversees the GIS efforts in AEP's Land Management Department.

Before the GIS, his department could either have the land surveyed or have the maps drawn by hand on U.S. Geological Survey (USGS) topographic maps. Each option had drawbacks. AEP wanted to avoid the up-front costs of surveying the land before deciding to sell it. Often with large tracts of land the survey team could not be scheduled for months, hindering a potential sale. Hand drawing maps on USGS topographic files was time-consuming, inaccurate, and redundant. Sometimes maps had to be redrawn or multiple copies made.

Williams maps property on a project basis usually when there is an impending sale or purchase. The utility needs a map drawn in four instances: the sale of property, sale of assets, granting of easements, and sale of mineral rights.

Williams especially likes the ability of GIS to integrate spatial and tabular data. "GIS is such an important communication tool," Williams said. "Not only can you map the property boundaries, you can analyze the attributes of the land." Land Management now keeps track of acreage, soil types, elevation, mineral content, and other attributes in an Oracle® database. The goal is to move all the paper documents online, map the property, and link it to the attributes so data can be viewed graphically with the GIS.

Computer mapping provided immediate benefits. "We were planning to sell a piece of timberland, but the cost of surveying the property would likely cancel any profit we made from the sale," explained Williams. So the field crew used the GPS features collected in ArcPad to complete a field survey, then mapped it with UCLID software's IcoMap for ArcGIS. "We were able to accurately map the property and make a profit," he said.

Williams found that IcoMap's unique technology for converting scanned documents into digital maps offers many benefits. He works an estimated 50- to 75-percent faster when he uses IcoMap on scanned deeds than if he keyed in the calls. IcoMap also has timesaving quality assurance features that enable users to edit individual lines.

IcoMap uses the survey measurements to draw COGO-accurate maps. Because IcoMap automatically enters the measurements, there is no risk of typing errors. Williams recently mapped a parcel with five hundred calls. A struggling economy may

American Electric Power uses GIS to manage property information. GIS analysis helps the company determine whether selling or keeping the land is more profitable.

tempt some to delay the important task of building a GIS. Yet Williams found GIS actually made his department more efficient and productive—just the ticket in competitive times.

He notes that GIS is also an effective decision-making tool. When AEP is considering expanding a plant's boundaries or building a new power plant, the boundary needs to be within a certain proximity to water for cooling. "First we find nearby streams and lakes to provide the water. Then we overlay environmentally protected areas," said Williams. "It helps us decide where to put the boundaries so they match the requirements but don't encroach on protected areas."

Williams expects to have all the Land Management records online in one year. After that, ESRI's ArcIMS will make the GIS accessible via the company's intranet, giving other departments access to accurate information regarding the company's land. With his GIS efforts, Williams is continuing the AEP tradition of innovation and efficiency. ⊙

ADDITIONAL BENEFITS

GIS takes on crime fighting role in Virginia

SECTOR *Law enforcement/Criminal justice*
INDUSTRY *Government*

Jess Hansen
GIS Manager, Anderson & Associates
www.andassoc.com
Story by Jennifer Dobson

Wise County, Virginia, is contributing to a growing trend in crime fighting. In fall 2002, a guilty verdict was handed down in a criminal trial, and it was the first time that GIS had been used in a Wise County court case.

Prosecutors charged the defendant, Harless Rose, with the October 5, 2000, robbery and murder of Tim Hughes. Hughes, along with two clerks, had been making a night deposit at a local bank when a masked gunman robbed him. After the criminal ran off, Hughes followed and was shot twice.

Rose became a suspect in the crime when authorities matched his DNA to DNA found in a ski mask left near the scene of the shooting. This piece of evidence became an integral part of the prosecution's case. The police used tracking dogs and eyewitness accounts to trace the path the defendant ran. The jury needed to know the distance of the path that the murderer ran because the time it took to run that distance would discredit Rose's alibi.

Coeburn Police Sergeant Willie Stout used Wise County's WebGIS site to show the jury the suspect's path as he fled the scene. According to Stout, "[The WebGIS] was able to give us distances that, because of the terrain, you couldn't normally measure with any real degree of accuracy."

The prosecutor, Gary Gilliam, the Assistant Wise County Commonwealth Attorney, said, "GIS really helped in this case." A videotape and map of the perpetrator's path helped the prosecution, but GIS showed the jury the approximate distance of the run. According to Gilliam, it "was impressive to the jury."

Jessica Swinney, of the Wise County Circuit Court Clerk's Office, testified about the accuracy of the maps and the measurements on the maps, which helped to discount Rose's alibi that he could not have been at the scene of the crime because he was with some of his friends who could substantiate this.

The potential for GIS in law enforcement is limitless. According to Jess Hansen, the GIS manager of Anderson & Associates' Tennessee office, "the visual properties and analytical tools in a GIS are proving to be essential for not only solving crimes but also for improving response times and preventing crimes in the first place." Geography plays an important role in law enforcement and criminal justice. Response capabilities often rely on a variety of data from multiple agencies and multiple sources. The ability to access and process information quickly while displaying it in a spatial and visual medium gives agencies the ability to allocate resources quickly and more effectively. In the mission-critical nature of law enforcement, information about the location of a crime, incident, suspect, or victim is often crucial in determining the manner and size of the response. ⊙

ADDITIONAL BENEFITS

Making roads safer in Colorado

In May 2000, the Boulder County Road Maintenance Department in Colorado began implementing a new method of sign inventory maintenance using ArcPad, ESRI's mobile GIS technology. Previously, keeping the sign database current and accurate was a problem because of a time delay in acquiring the daily employee time sheet data and then entering that information into the sign database. The time sheets log the Boulder County Sign Shop employees' daily activities and contain information such as a sign bar code number and what work was performed. A unique bar code number is assigned to each sign, and if an employee entered the wrong bar code number, the data would be associated with the wrong sign in the database. These types of errors in the updating process required periodic, expensive, and time-consuming GPS sign resurveys to keep the database accurate and current.

SECTOR *Public works*
INDUSTRY *Government*
John Mosher
Boulder County, Colorado, Road Maintenance Department
www.boulder.co.us

With the new method, Sign Shop personnel carry a pocket PC containing an accurate and current digital map of more than seven thousand road signs with all the necessary information about each sign including type and location. Employees update information about an existing sign in the database while looking at the sign, and missing or incorrect signs have become much easier to locate and replace. Roadside sign inspections are more complete and accurate, and mistakes that an employee notes in either the inspection procedure or the information in the existing database are corrected.

The method significantly reduced employee mileage for sign replacement and inspection, as well as paperwork and data entry errors. The Road Maintenance Sign Shop has three sign technicians using this system, resulting in a savings of one to two hours a day per employee. Employees can spend this time performing more field maintenance, increasing overall productivity. Time savings for GIS personnel due to the elimination of data entry from paperwork are approximately two hours per week. Total savings are more than $20,000 per year, and one of the unexpected benefits is that county road signs are now extremely accurate, providing the public with the safety level that was originally engineered into the roads.

Using ArcPad with a pocket PC supplies inexpensive, accurate, timely, and reliable information updates while supplying users with the necessary information in the field to perform their tasks at the highest level of accuracy and efficiency. ⊙

In Boulder County, the road maintenance department uses ArcPad to maintain its sign inventory, which has reduced employee mileage, paperwork, and data-entry errors.

ADDITIONAL BENEFITS

Setting standards for accuracy

SECTOR Public works
INDUSTRY Government

Patrick J. Bresnahan, PhD
Geographic Information Officer, Richland County, South Carolina
www.richlandmaps.com

One principle of the GIS implementation plan at Richland County, South Carolina, requires data to be maintained through standardized business practices. When the county GIS program began in 1999, several departments jointly developed a strategy to review permit applications while aiding data maintenance.

The initial phase of the program included a $265,000 contract to install 225 new survey monuments in the county.

Within the new storm water permit program for land development, the county required developers to submit design drawings and plans in digital format tied to the State Plane coordinate system. The county could then review proposed development within the physical context of the built environment with GIS applications.

The Planning and Public Works Departments worked with the GIS Division within the Information Technology Department to establish CAD layer definitions and standards to be included in the requirement. They held several workshops for local engineers and surveyors to introduce the new requirements. The first seminar focused on storm water design and permitting and introduced the concept of digital data submission.

The second seminar included a session on State Plane mapping presented by a national figure in surveying as well as an equipment display of aircraft and sensors used to collect data for the county. A follow-up seminar for technicians introduced CAD layer management to meet the new county requirement. As an incentive for professionals to attend, each county seminar offered free continuing education credits required by state licensing.

During the series of seminars, the county also met with the local engineers and surveyors to address technical concerns. To discourage resistance to the requirements, the county rejected submitted plans that did not adhere to the standards. The digital data is now flowing.

Richland County began a survey monument densification program to help local surveyors and engineers reference the State Plane coordinate system.

The initial phase of the program included a $265,000 contract to install 225 new survey monuments in the county. The county chose the monument sites to provide control for the developing areas within the 770 square miles of Richland County. The county excluded areas such as the capital city (Columbia), Fort Jackson, and the Congaree Swamp National Monument from the project because federal law bars development in protected areas and the county does not manage permitting on the military base or in the city. The county submitted the survey monument network to the United States National Geodetic Survey to be "blue booked" and maintained.

Data for monuments in the Richland County network are available on the county GIS Web site (*www.richlandmaps.com*). County personnel or local

surveyors will install new monuments and add monuments to the network on an as-needed basis as land development continues.

Richland County ties data to a common reference by combining digital data submission requirements and establishing a survey monument network. The expenditures for the training seminars, guest speakers, and the monument network have begun to pay off in the quality of data submitted to the county. Because plans are submitted in standard digital format and tied to the State Plane coordinate system, the Public Works Department performs a technical review and runs watershed models within the GIS without having to redraft plans or rubber sheet scanned plans into a GIS layer. The receipt of as-built digital files for each development aids the maintenance of county GIS layers. The county will not accept dedication of roads and drainage for subdivisions or issue a certificate of occupancy for commercial development until Public Work receives the digital as-built files.

Judging from the first few months of data submission, the cost of changing the way the county and local professionals do business and installing a survey monument network will be a small price to pay for increased efficiency in plan review, more accurate data, and improved data maintenance. ⊙

In Richland County, South Carolina, developers submit digital design drawings and plans that are tied to the State Plane coordinate system. The county began a survey monument densification program to assist local surveyors and engineers in referencing the State Plane coordinate system.

Costa Rican city gets back on track

SECTOR *Cadastral*
INDUSTRY *Government (International)*

Sebastian Salazar
Agronomical Tropical Center for Research and Teaching
www.catie.ac.cr

Turrialba, a small city located on the Caribbean side of Costa Rica, is sixty-four kilometers southeast of the country's capital, San José. Home to approximately thirty-four thousand people, Turrialba's economy is dominated by agriculture—coffee, sugar cane, and macadamia nut production. The Rawlings baseball factory and ConAir processing plant are also located in Turrialba.

Since the early 1900s, Turrialba's municipal government has collected tax revenue and provided basic services such as drinking water, public lighting, and sewage services. In 1998, the city's database showed that approximately twelve thousand of the city's residents received services, but only about 20 percent of these residents paid for services.

Insufficient revenue during the 1990s made it difficult for the city to provide basic services. The widespread belief that the city did not oblige residents to pay for services such as drinking water and street cleaning was part of the problem. In addition, poor tax collection methods and the failure to raise taxes limited revenues caused services to further deteriorate and increased the city's deficit.

Before 1998, the city stored tax collection information in tabular form in a FoxPro® database on a single 486 computer without a backup system. This database contained serious errors in addresses, names, and identification numbers. The lack of reliable original information made correcting these errors difficult, and this system could only retrieve and print outstanding accounts one at a time. Citizens, critical of the poor state of municipal services, expressed their dissatisfaction, which tarnished the city's image.

Coupled with poor communication between city departments, rapid growth within the city during the late 1990s exacerbated problems. Because files were often out of date or incomplete, the tax, urban, and real estate tax departments had little confidence in these records. The city was collecting less than $1,500 per day in taxes.

The city's board and the mayor recognized that GIS could be used to efficiently identify taxpayers and link tabular data in the municipal database to graphic information. The city began the municipal GIS (MGIS) project in January 1998. Working

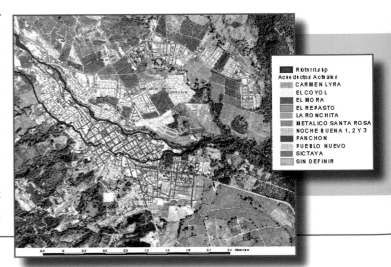

with the GIS laboratory at the Agronomical Tropical Center for Research and Teaching, the city obtained and geocoded external data sets, verified information in the new database, and developed query and reporting tools. By the end of 1998, the center had organized the database and linked graphic and text information about taxpayers for the system to identify service users by name, identity card, parcel number, or neighborhood. A MapObjects® application handles geographic information, and a Delphi® 3 application handles the accounting database. A Pentium® II computer serves this information through an intranet to computers in the municipal buildings.

With MGIS, city departments can immediately access current information that allows staff members to provide friendly and fast service to the public. Because MGIS integrates tabular data with graphic information, staff can centrally access information

One year after the city implemented MGIS, tax revenue nearly doubled, climbing from $376,000 to $611,300.

relating to a service user with a mouse click. This information includes geographic location, personal identification number, a description of the property and the services received, and information on the state of repair. The city also can obtain a complete and detailed breakdown of customer accounts.

One year after the city implemented MGIS, tax revenue nearly doubled, climbing from $376,000 to $611,300. Projected revenue for 2001 was nearly $1.2 million, an increase of almost 300 percent. For the first time, the city projected revenue to exceed outlays and looked forward to retiring a $160,714 deficit, paying the annual salary raise for workers, and having a surplus of $15,000. ◉

Staff within the City of Turrialba, Costa Rica, have immediate access to the municipal database with the click of a mouse.

Tax revenue in this Costa Rican city nearly doubled one year after the GIS implementation.

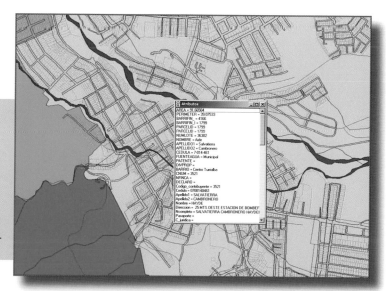

Uncovering inequitable assessments

SECTOR Media
INDUSTRY Business

Bill Bush
Reporter, *Columbus Dispatch*
www.dispatch.com

Local governments and school districts derive a large share of operating funds from real estate taxes. Each year, property owners are taxed based on simple math—the value of their property multiplied by the local tax rate as set by local legislators and school boards. The higher the value of a property, the higher its tax bill will be. Similar properties are supposed to have similar assessed values. Even though government officials and agencies establish formulas, procedures, and systems to try to ensure equity, owners frequently appeal what they believe are unfair assessments.

The reporter used GIS to discover unequal tax burdens, something no one else in the county had done before.

At the *Columbus Dispatch* newspaper, a reporter wanted to dig deeper into residential property tax equity in Columbus and surrounding Franklin County, Ohio. The newspaper requested the assessment data from the Franklin County Auditor's Office, which provided the data in dBASE® tables on CD–ROM for less than $25. The data included fields of information such as location, sale price, assessment, and sale date.

The database itself was complex, with a common fourteen-character identification number linking approximately twenty tables. The *Dispatch* reporter needed additional data about property transactions between unaffiliated parties from the state of Ohio, which he obtained and merged with the auditor data using Microsoft Access.

At the same time the reporter obtained the data from the county auditor, he and a *Dispatch* editor saw an ArcView demonstration at a reporters' conference. They realized they could compare GIS to a database manager with a map. GIS can query data and show the results on a map or in a table. Consequently, after the conference, the *Dispatch* newsroom bought ArcView, and the reporter used it for the property tax investigative story.

With the assessment data and GIS, the reporter had to obtain the map layer files for the analysis. He got those in ArcView shapefile format from the Franklin County Development Department's Web site. The parcel files also included a unique identification number for each parcel. The reporter used GIS to discover unequal tax burdens, something no one else in the county had done before. When he finished compiling and querying the data, he saw an unmistakable pattern. Properties in upper income neighborhoods tended to be uniformly assessed at values less than the selling price. Properties in lower income area had less consistent patterns, but clearly had a number of overassessed properties.

In its two-part series about residential assessments, the *Dispatch* reported that the homes of inner-city families were more likely to be overappraised than the homes of upper-income suburbanites. One-fourth of all the inner-city homeowners paid more than 110 percent of their share of the tax burden. The *Dispatch* published two maps—one that showed the properties with high over-assessments and a second that showed the properties with high under-assessments.

Government officials reacted. A state representative whose district covered part of inner-city Columbus said he would mail his constituents information about the assessment problems. The county auditor ordered his staff to review records for the parcels identified in the newspaper stories as highly over- or under-assessed. He said the staff would send letters to homeowners with apparent inaccurate assessments and suggest that they file appeals.

As a result of the *Columbus Dispatch* investigation, the auditor ordered the independent appraisal firm hired by the office to investigate the assessments of four thousand residential properties with sale values that diverged widely from their assessed values. His office also sent 280,000 brochures to property owners that explained real estate taxes. The auditor later told the *Dispatch* that the mailing had prompted 3,800 additional calls from property owners.

By using GIS, the reporter graphically showed the areas of over- and under-assessment. This helped the county government collect property taxes that accurately reflected what the property owners owed. ⊙

Adapted from *Mapping the News: Case Studies in GIS and Journalism* by David Herzog, ESRI Press 2003, with permission from Bill Bush, reporter for the *Columbus Dispatch, www.dispatch.com.*

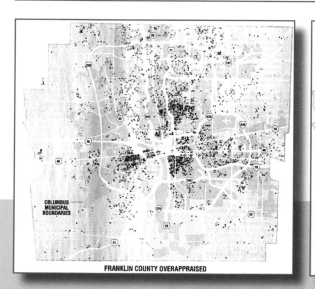

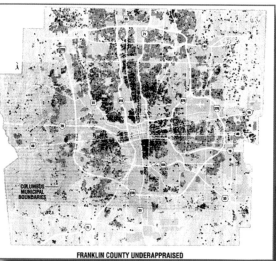

The *Columbus Dispatch* ran maps with stories about unfair assessments. One map showed the properties that had been greatly under-assessed, and the other showed properties that had been greatly over-assessed.

ADDITIONAL BENEFITS

Eco-friendly pest eradication is efficient

SECTOR *Health and human services*
INDUSTRY *Government*

Dave Lawson
Assistant Director, Norfolk County, Massachusetts, Mosquito Control Project
users.rcn.com/ncmcp

The Norfolk County Mosquito Control Project serves twenty-five towns southwest of Boston, Massachusetts. For many years the project has sprayed aerial larvicides in a handful of towns that provided additional funding to support the applications. The desire to provide environmentally sensitive and highly effective mosquito control motivated the participating towns. Aerial applications of Bti, an extremely low toxicity larvicide, provided the desired results.

The whole process was approximately 40 percent more time efficient using the computerized maps.

In 2000, environmental pressure to reduce ground-based adulticide applications prompted the district to internally finance aerial larvicide applications for the entire district. The first year succeeded to a degree, despite glitches. The helicopter contractors were required to fly using paper maps and locate wetlands visually. GPS navigation and navigation software enabled helicopter pilots to see the application swath locations on a screen, but assessments of the wetlands' boundaries were entirely visual. The location of the Bti applications largely depended on visual judgment of the wetlands' boundaries. Ground-based post-treatment surveys revealed that many wetlands did not receive complete coverage.

To help resolve these shortcomings, the district purchased ArcGIS. The district downloaded wetland locations from the Massachusetts GIS database *(www.state.ma.us/mgis/massgis.htm)*. The district analyzed the data using aerial photographs to eliminate wetlands that were either too small for the helicopters to efficiently treat or were assessed as nonmosquito breeding wetlands. The district was divided into regions based on proximity to a helicopter landing site, and the wetland data for each region was converted to files that the helicopter navigation system could read.

This enabled the helicopter pilots to fly directly to a wetland by GPS navigation and perform complete coverage of the wetland without having to rely on visual assessments. The wetland delineation appeared on a screen in the helicopter. When the pilots crossed the wetland boundary on the screen, they were also crossing the wetland boundary on the ground. After the larvicide application, application data was downloaded and converted back to shape-files and re-entered into the district's ArcGIS maps. Staff members could view map coverages, provide accurate acreage figures, and access data at all times.

According to Dave Lawson, assistant director for the Norfolk County Mosquito Control Project, "ArcGIS provided a method for using accurate wet-land delineation maps, a fail-safe way for the helicopter pilots to locate and accurately treat the specified wetlands, and a way to integrate our ground-based mosquito survey databases to the maps. The whole process was approximately 40 percent more time efficient using the computerized maps, and though we can't put a figure on it, we know it is more efficient in accurately treating the wetlands.

"This leads to savings in work-hours and better mosquito control for the public. As our familiariza-tion with the whole process increases, we hope to make it even more efficient." ⊙

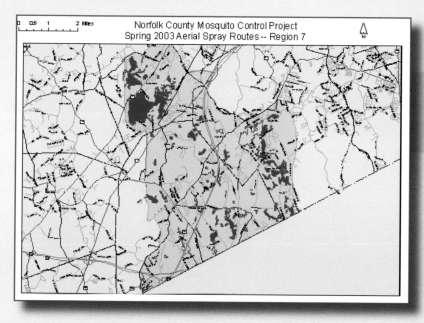

In Massachusetts, the Norfolk County Mosquito Control Project uses ArcGIS to locate wetlands for mosquito spraying.

ADDITIONAL BENEFITS

INCREASE PRODUCTIVITY

The ratio that measures how well businesses convert inputted resources—labor, materials, machines—into goods and services is called productivity. From a product or service perspective, improvements in productivity result from a measurable increase in the output of product or service level. Labor productivity refers to the relationship between output and the labor time used to generate that output. Increases in productivity are typically reported as a percentage increase in yield or via a ratio of output per hour.

Businesses have long viewed improved productivity as a way to beat the competition and increase profits. Government organizations adopted new ways to increase productivity to meet accountability and performance demands from the public. The public- and private-sector view improved productivity as critical to the management of time, labor, and costs. Management constantly weighs new approaches to increase productivity. These methods have evolved to include solutions such as employee motivation, improved equipment and technology, and ergonomics.

As labor and economic resources dwindle and older procedures offer diminishing returns, organizations seek new opportunities to improve performance. Just as managers view GIS as a tool to increase efficiency in re-engineering processes, they are looking at the roles geography and GIS play in daily operations.

Compelling evidence shows that GIS has transformed the way we work. Precision agricultural techniques have helped produce superior crop yields, using GIS to analyze the impact geography has on soil, climate, weather, water quality and availability, crop rotation, and terrain. With GIS, sales organizations have realigned territories based on potential customers. With government, GIS technology has proved itself as a powerful tool to improve work flows and broaden the scope of e-government. Mobile GIS solutions have also increased performance rates of public works professionals in data collection and asset management.

Plum Creek Timber boosts parcel mapping productivity

SECTOR *Forestry*
INDUSTRY *Natural resources*

Paige Medlin
UCLID Software, LLC
www.uclid.com

Plum Creek Timber, the second largest private timberland owner in the United States, manages eight million acres of forest. Plum Creek's holdings are in the Pacific Northwest, across the south, and along the east coast. The forests are filled with a rich mix of Douglas-fir, hemlock, pine, spruce, and cedar. As land managers, Plum Creek actively protects the land from erosion, maintains recreation areas, preserves landscape aesthetics, and provides natural wildlife habitat.

Plum Creek also manufactures wood products, develops real estate, and operates a coal mine in West Virginia. Its nine mills in Montana produce high-performance plywood and lumber favored by do-it-yourself home builders. To reduce waste, the company uses residuals of lumber and plywood production for medium-density fiberboard—homogeneous panels for furniture components and cabinet doors.

Government leaders, the national media, and environmentalists recognize Plum Creek for its scientific accomplishments and environmental practices. Successful in business, its work has advanced forestry

science. Plum Creek credits many of its accomplishments to state-of-the-art technology such as GIS.

Plum Creek and other timber companies face tough decisions that affect their bottom lines as well as the environment. Before taking any action, the company evaluates neighboring lands and the history of a timber stand. For example, a forester would not clear-cut land that borders a stream or wildlife area. The history of a timber stand includes seeding, fertilization, and harvest schedules. Knowing the history helps keep harvesting and reforestation on schedule and increases efficiency.

With so many details to track spatially and temporally, GIS is a natural fit for forestry. John Vona, senior GIS analyst for Plum Creek Timber, oversees the Integrated Forest Management System, a desktop GIS application that enables foresters to manage and analyze volumes of timberland data. The system was built in 1997 with ESRI ArcInfo and Avenue™ scripts; the data is stored in an Oracle database. Using this system, a forester can quickly run a query and map areas due for fertilization or planting. Or users can simply select a timber stand to review its history and future plans.

Current, accurate data is the lifeblood of a GIS. An up-to-date, reliable database is essential to produce accurate reports. Field crews record

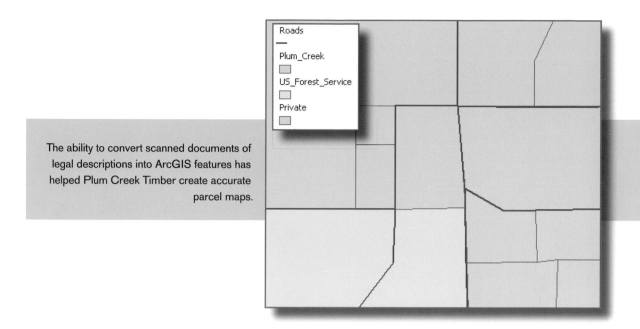

The ability to convert scanned documents of legal descriptions into ArcGIS features has helped Plum Creek Timber create accurate parcel maps.

information primarily through ArcPad. They enter field data and upload it to the database, which saves time. No one needs to transcribe field notes, and it eliminates lag time between recording the data and updating the database.

From the forest floor to the boardroom

The volumes of field data become invaluable to boardroom executives. The office of Corporate and Operations Support analyzes costs and efficiencies to achieve maximum timber growth and financial returns. Analysts use the Integrated Forest Management System to report the cost of planting, fertilizing, and harvesting. The system stores tabular data that lets management track cash flow and revenue projections.

While foresters concentrate on harvest planning, accountants focus on tax planning. Since 1999 the company has operated as a real estate investment trust, combining the capital of many investors to acquire and own real estate such as timberlands. Because Plum Creek draws most of its income from timber sales, which is treated as capital gain income, rigorous accounting guidelines apply—guidelines that required Vona to recreate the parcel layer of the GIS. ➤

IcoMap ... increases parcel-mapping productivity for the average user by approximately 84 percent.

In January 2003, the accounting department ordered Vona to reconcile the GIS acres with the legal records of land sales in Plum Creek's busy real estate division. "Small parcels of land are constantly changing hands," said Vona. Plum Creek frequently encounters requests from a highway department for a five-acre right-of-way, but it also has twenty-thousand-acre land sales. Each sale has a property legal description, and accounting needed maps of these descriptions.

Vona first gathered the legal descriptions for land sales since 2001, a stack of paper nearly a foot high. With so many legal descriptions, Vona worried how long it would take to finish the job. His experience in coordinate geometry (COGO) software language offered little comfort as he faced the prospect of spending a month mapping legal descriptions.

An article in an e-mail newsletter, *Spatial News*, which featured IcoMap, intrigued Vona. Developed by UCLID Software, IcoMap is a parcel mapping extension for ESRI ArcGIS that increases parcel-mapping productivity for the average user by approximately 84 percent. IcoMap has a solid ten-key COGO package. But Vona was sold by IcoMap's ability to convert scanned documents into ArcGIS features.

Vona scanned his stack of property legal descriptions and then used IcoMap to create the parcel geometry. The survey measurements are used to create the line work, so the result is COGO-accurate. IcoMap uses a point-and-click interface, which is much faster than keying the data. "IcoMap saved our bacon," said Vona. "I thought it would take me a month; instead it took me about a week."

As a result, Plum Creek cut two hundred parcels from its land base. Vona credited IcoMap. "It was bug-free, easy to learn, and everyone is happy with the results." Plum Creek found its in-house Integrated Forest Management system indispensable, and new technologies have increased productivity in the GIS department. GIS tools enabled accounting to satisfy an important IRS requirement. ⊙

Without IcoMap	Using IcoMap	Total time savings
One month	One week	30–40 percent

ADDITIONAL BENEFITS

Streamlining vehicle dispatching with ArcLogistics Route

GoodCents Solutions, a small electrical firm headquartered in Stone Mountain, Georgia, installs surge-protection equipment and load management devices for electrical appliances. As a contract service provider to utility companies in five states, GoodCents Solutions serves mostly residential customers who use energy-saving, cost-saving devices to cycle off their appliances during peak use and peak cost hours.

Until recently, GoodCents Solutions dispatchers used a manual system of spreadsheets, ZIP Code lists, map books, and wall maps to locate hundreds of service orders; assign each order to a service technician; and ultimately design a set of five routes (representing the following week's work) for each technician. The manual routing and scheduling process took time. Dispatchers typically spent three to four work-days per week to build routes for their twelve service technicians.

As the company won contracts for new projects, managers quickly realized that continuing to rely on manual routing methods was simply not practical. Some service orders also required set appointments, further complicating an already laborious process.

"In the past, we manually sorted our service orders by ZIP Code and then assigned technicians to a cluster of ZIP Codes," said Mike Whalen, GoodCents Solutions vice president of operations. "This system was inefficient, especially considering that we now have some projects with fifteen to twenty technicians. We needed a better routing system—one that would speed up the route planning process."

SECTOR *Logistics and fleet management*
INDUSTRY *Transportation*

Wilbur Blackman
Project Manager, GoodCents Solutions
www.goodcents.com

GoodCents Solutions contacted Herb Rawling from Mapping Technologies International, Inc., in Moorestown, New Jersey, an ESRI business partner, and received a demonstration of ArcLogistics Route. "We were impressed with how fast we could bring our service orders into the system and build routes," said GoodCents dispatcher Beth Allen.

> *"It used to take most of the week to route the next week's work for twelve technicians. Now it takes a day or less to route twenty technicians."* —*Wilbur Blackman*

A key software feature, the ability to decode service orders, greatly reduced the amount of time spent routing. When orders are imported into ArcLogistics Route, the street address for each order is geocoded, or matched, against the underlying street database. If a match is not found, the dispatcher uses an interactive map to place an electronic pushpin at the correct location for that service order. The dispatcher saves the exact service location for future use. The system is a huge time saver for GoodCents Solutions because dispatchers often cannot route service orders on the first pass-through.

ArcLogistics Route easily handles service orders that require an appointment time, which helps GoodCents Solutions streamline the route planning process. The software automatically takes the appointment time into account when the company builds routes Also, when a technician is scheduled for a day off, a dispatcher simply locks out the vehicle assigned to that technician to prevent it from being used.

"It used to take most of the week to route the next week's work for twelve technicians. Now it takes a day or less to route twenty technicians," said Wilbur Blackman, project manager at GoodCents. ⊙

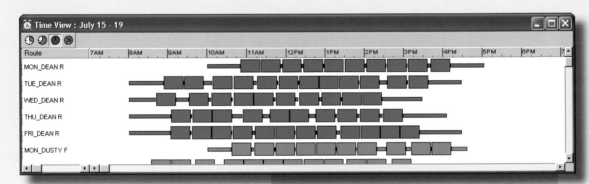

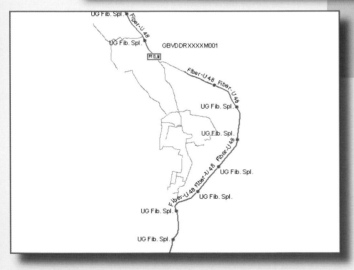

GoodCents Solutions, a small Georgia electrical firm, reduced time spent routing service orders with ArcLogistics Route.

ADDITIONAL BENEFITS

Technology helps win market share

In today's global economy, the lines between industries and countries blur as research crosses boundaries. Global competition, rapid technological advances, and legislative reform are driving the communications world toward fast-paced changes. To gain a competitive edge, telecommunication companies such as Reliance Infocomm Limited, based in Mumbai, India, have embraced GIS as a technology tool to help it survive, compete, and win market share.

A new carrier in the recently deregulated Indian telecommunications market, Reliance Infocomm is building a vast broadband network and Internet protocol backbone to connect India's top 582 cities with more than sixty thousand route kilometers of fiber that will offer terabit capacity. After completing the network, Reliance will offer customers a full range of services, including national coverage, fixed line and mobile national long distance, and international long distance that offers data and image services.

In May 2001, ESRI's Professional Services Division began working with Reliance Infocomm to define and start an enterprise-wide GIS to manage its telecommunications network and associated land base for its service area covering India. The enterprise GIS, jointly developed with business partner MESA Solutions, Inc., provides Reliance with a centralized corporate record of land base and facility data. The GIS enables Reliance users to produce and maintain a comprehensive geodatabase containing network facilities, customer locations, buildings, roads, sales, marketing, and boundary data. Data

SECTOR Telecommunication
INDUSTRY Utilities (International)
A. Ramanathan
Reliance Infocomm
www.ril.com/eportal/home.jsp

is stored in a seamless geodatabase using ArcSDE and Oracle. The spatial data is available to various departments within Reliance using ArcGIS clients or via the corporate intranet.

> *"The implementation of GIS technology enables Reliance Infocomm to provide the highest level of customer service available in the industry." —A. Ramanathan*

"The implementation of GIS technology enables Reliance Infocomm to provide the highest level of customer service available in the industry," said A. Ramanathan, Reliance's vice president of projects. "We anticipate improving productivity and overall efficiency through streamlined work processes. The system eliminates the need for multiple applications and data formats and provides an open, easy-to-use platform for our staff."

The enterprise system gives Reliance open data access, which has increased staff productivity, provided rapid response when network outages occur, and ensured that the company gains a competitive advantage in its market. ⊙

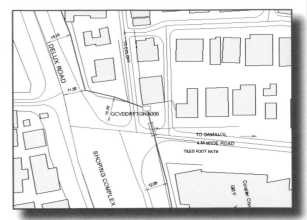

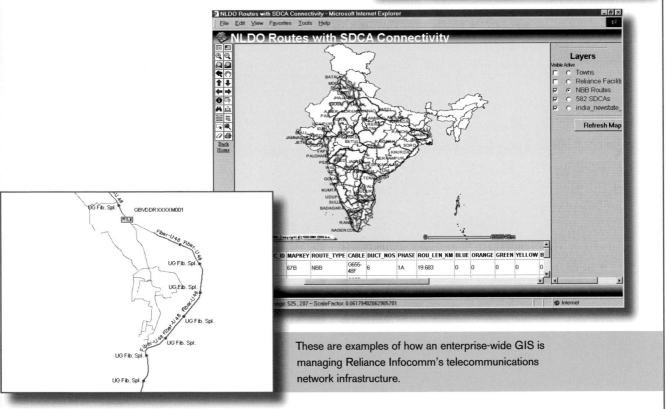

These are examples of how an enterprise-wide GIS is managing Reliance Infocomm's telecommunications network infrastructure.

ADDITIONAL BENEFITS

INCREASE COMMUNICATION AND COLLABORATION

Lack of communication and collaboration results in system breakdowns. Using GIS as a communication and collaboration tool integrates the technology into the business work flow. A GIS can assemble and share information among various departments and present it in a way that staff, external stakeholders, business partners, clients, and the public can understand and use.

An organization needs to communicate effectively to meet its goals. Communication increases our understanding of business problems and possible solutions. As an organization moves forward, presentations communicate a confident understanding of the issues to colleagues. While traditional communication methods offer reports and business statistics, GIS offers a graphic solution. GIS is renowned for conveying information clearly. Its maps visually explain and portray simple and complex subjects.

In addition to maps, the software produces charts and reports from geographic queries and helps provide insight into spatial anomalies through geostatistical analyses, three-dimensional viewpoints, virtual interaction, and interactive mapping.

Multi-agency task forces exemplify this process when they swing into action during an emergency. GIS integrates multiple databases for decision makers to address resource distribution and disaster mitigation and recovery.

GIS can engage internal and external users in an organization's business work flow by facilitating access to central and local data. This common knowledge base helps stakeholders make informed, cooperative business decisions.

Enhanced communication and collaboration are often unintended but welcome benefits that organizations realize after they develop a successful enterprise-wide GIS.

Health care application gives the public a voice

SECTOR *Health and human service*
INDUSTRY *Government*

Scott Christman
California Office of Statewide Health Planning and
Development Information Technology Services
www.oshpd.state.ca.us

The state of California, through the Office of Statewide Health Planning and Development (OSHPD), works to ensure equal access to health care for all Californians. In that spirit, OSHPD is responsible for addressing the misdistribution of health care services throughout the state. OSHPD delineates geographic boundaries within California and then identifies areas that do not meet medical service needs. The state has been divided into roughly five hundred medical service study areas (MSSAs) for health care analysis and needs assessment purposes. The MSSA boundaries determine the amount of potential state and federal funds, and other resources that health care providers will receive in each service area.

The U.S. Department of Health and Human Services designates medically underserved areas, medically underserved populations, and health professional shortage areas. Designating them accurately depends on the geographic reconfiguration of study area boundaries after each census.

The reconfiguration process incorporates information such as demographics, income levels, race, and ethnicity to determine community and neighborhood boundaries. They are also used to separate urban and rural areas based on population densities.

Determining boundaries

Many states use county lines as boundaries to determine study areas. This does not accurately capture the distribution of health care resources in California. As the largest county in the contiguous United States, San Bernardino County includes densely populated urban areas and many sparsely populated areas that qualify for rural health funds. To adequately assess need and distribute resources, the state must accurately configure subcounty and subcity study areas. For this purpose, GIS plays a major role in determining MSSAs.

"Our use of GIS," said Scott Christman, GIS coordinator for OSHPD, "has recently focused on the identification and configuration of primary health care service areas in California. The MSSAs are an aggregation of contiguous census tracts, defined by a set of guidelines authorized by our state Health Manpower Policy Commission. The California MSSAs are also recognized by the federal Department of Health and Human Services for approving designations of various health care shortages.

"The criteria for these designations include variables such as poverty population, senior population, physician-to-population ratio, and infant mortality tabulated according to the geographic

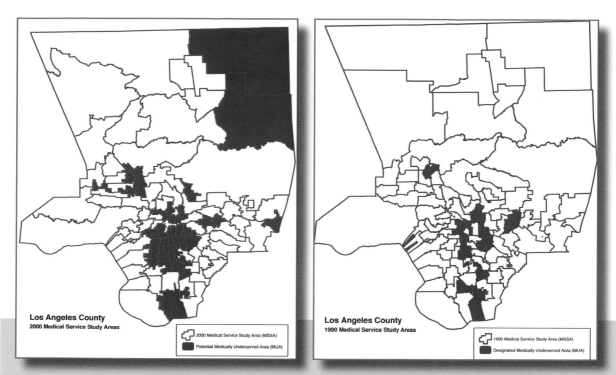

The California Office of Statewide Health Planning and Development uses GIS to identify areas where there is an unmet need for medical services.

boundaries established through the MSSA process. We recognized that if these variables are calculated dynamically using GIS districting tools, we could actually optimize the delineation of underserved areas and maximize the potential for federal funds awarded to the providers in these communities of need.

"With the support of VESTRA Resources, Inc., of Redding, California, we have been using ArcGIS Desktop and the Districting for ArcGIS add-on as we conduct interactive community meetings in each county with primary care safety net providers and other health care community stakeholders. We reconfigure these areas with Census 2000 geography and data. The resulting MSSA geography

is data driven and community based, and we are confident that our complete statewide MSSA boundaries will be infused with local knowledge of health care service areas."

According to Deborah Wong, GIS project manager at OSHPD, the project benefits from GIS in many ways. It adds value to existing OSHPD technology projects and programs by enabling widespread use of geographic analysis tools and by providing more meaningful analysis results in an understandable format. Staff can redirect its efforts from simple data dissemination and summarization to comprehensive health care analysis, evaluation, visualization, and planning, which is a principal business goal for OSHPD. ➤

Using ArcGIS and districting tools, OSHPD completed the Los Angeles County 2000 reconfiguration in less than five months, with only eleven community meetings.

The GIS also serves to do the following:

- Reduce time spent looking up and plotting the addresses of facility-related information on a map.
- Provide easy access to shared, consistent digital map data sets that are commonly used throughout the organization, other state departments, and external stakeholders.
- Improve work flow by providing more complete spatial analysis capabilities to reduce time spent doing repetitive, human-intensive analysis tasks.
- Provide easily accessible, geographically referenced information to individuals and organizations to help answer important questions regarding trends and changes in delivery and organization of health care services, facilitate planning and distribution of resources to address issues of disparity in health care access, understand and develop strategies for health care delivery issues for vulnerable populations, and track health care facility information over time for health care trend analysis.
- Improve the visual quality and interpretability of health care information analysis presented to decision makers and the public.
- Enable data users to relate and link health care facility utilization, community benefits, and financial and patient-level data contained within the OSHPD health care data stores through common, compatible data elements including geographic location.

- Contribute and share important health care information with other organizations and the public by adhering to the guiding principles of statewide e-government and GIS initiatives.

OSHPD uses GIS to compile, analyze, and display geographic data in support of study area boundaries, allowing department staff to run queries on topics ranging from demographics to distance to accurately represent the community within the geographic boundaries.

Productive community meetings

Following each MSSA reconfiguration community meeting, the new study area boundaries and associated demographic data are presented to members of the community and health care stakeholders. Through the community meeting process, OSHPD gathers valuable information that would not otherwise be known. For instance, sometimes patients base their choice of hospital not on proximity but on religious affiliation. Some people may be more willing to travel longer distances to a familiar hospital. Community meetings further the department's understanding of local health care communities and lead to more efficient resource allocation.

The community meetings also provide the local stakeholders with ready-to-use information. By simply bringing a laptop to the meetings OSHPD staff can present, update, and modify the data with the help of the community. Using the ArcGIS districting extension, their combined efforts can automatically and interactively delineate new study areas. All community meetings to date have

MSSA reconfiguration before GIS	MSSA reconfiguration after GIS
Paper maps, hand-drawn maps	Data rich GIS, digital mapping, mobile technology
Required several years and numerous meetings	Typically requires only one community meeting per county (Los Angeles County is an exception)
Expensive and time-consuming	An efficient public process supporting timely buy-in from community stakeholders
Funding authorities often overlook many underserved communities.	Comprehensive identification and recognition of underserved communities across the state
Designation caseload backlogged	Designation processes on faster track

ended with consensus among the stakeholders regarding the newly configured study area boundaries.

Completed MSSA plans are taken to a state commission for approval. The agency presents results with accurate information and complete consensus from the community, which simplifies the approval process and instills confidence in policy makers when allocating resources based on study-area boundaries. With an image based on consensus from each community, it becomes clear where additional resources are needed. The newly configured areas can qualify for a variety of state and federal funding opportunities according to different MSSA designations.

Before the GIS, the reconfiguration process required copying, cutting, and pasting paper maps. In areas not covered by maps, staff would trace AAA maps and draw in the census tract lines. They

taped completed maps to the wall. California MSSA reconfigurations consumed time and meetings. Los Angeles County took two years and twenty-six public meetings to complete the reconfiguration process after the 1990 Census. Using ArcGIS and districting tools, OSHPD completed the Los Angeles County 2000 reconfiguration in less than five months, with only eleven community meetings. "GIS technology supports community health needs assessment much more effectively than other methods of interpreting tabular data," said William H. Burnett, Senior Associate, Postsecondary Education Studies at OSHPD. "Most people can readily understand health care patterns when the information is presented spatially. It makes months of work disappear and years of insight come into view." ⊙

"Most people can readily understand health care patterns when the information is presented spatially. It makes months of work disappear and years of insight come into view."

William H. Burnett, Senior Associate, Postsecondary Education Studies at OSHPD

 ADDITIONAL BENEFITS

Managing Small Town, USA

SECTOR *Public works*
INDUSTRY *Government*

Marie Bishop
City of Bellingham, Washington
www.cob.org/cobweb/pw/eng/gis/index.htm

The city of Bellingham, Washington, like many other communities in the Northwest, has experienced unprecedented growth during the last decade. Bellingham developed its GIS because of the significant increase in utility customers and infrastructure and need to manage city growth. The Public Works Department and city GIS staff have developed a comprehensive GIS that instills confidence and pride. With the GIS, the city can respond to and serve its customers more efficiently as it continues to manage, develop, and plan for the future.

There are more than 58,000 parcels, 372 miles of water main, 308 miles of sewer main, 183 miles of storm water features, and dozens of additional mapped data sets.

Bellingham is located on the northern edge of Puget Sound in the northwest corner of Washington. The city provides water, sewer, and storm water utility service to its 69,260 residents and additional service to a large urban growth area.

The city's GIS staff maintains all the parcel, water, sewer, and storm infrastructure data located in an area of more than 60 square miles. There are more than 58,000 parcels, 372 miles of water main, 308 miles of sewer main, 183 miles of storm water features, and dozens of additional mapped data sets. Bellingham has accurately collected new and many existing utility infrastructure locations using survey-grade GPS since 1998. The combination of the GPS and an expansive city cadastral survey system has provided a basis for a continually expanding and accurate parcel and utility mapping base.

Achieving accurate links

Initially, the Bellingham intended its GIS to be a geographic or mapping reference for the array of tabular data used throughout the city. To accomplish this, Bellingham needed its parcel data to accurately reference the county assessor's tabular information record by record. Property ownership, value, deed description, and land-use information is essential to land-use planning, storm-water utility billing, and

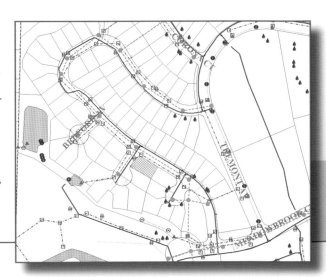

customer service. The city's Information Technology Services Department arranged and developed regular weekly update from the county assessor. GIS staff developed a record checking and review process to keep mapped property information current.

Next, the city linked its utility structure spatial data to its tabular asset database, the Hansen maintenance management system. This accomplishment involved the arduous task of matching thousands of sewer and water asset records in the maintenance management system to a mapped location in the GIS.

In 1999, the city expanded its vision for the GIS to provide a robust decision-making and customer service application. The basic design interconnected the GIS so that a user could have one piece of information (e.g., address, parcel or utility account number, or nearest intersection) and find and access all other related information. At that time, many of the desired data sets were in stand-alone flat files with no links to a mapped record, and in some cases the flat files did not have a geographic description to use as a link.

One-stop information retrieval

This new vision of the Bellingham GIS required a process of identifying all of the data sources desired for a potential customer transaction. After identifying all data sources, the city designed an overall data model using identified data sources. The city has an advantage—a staff well-rounded in its knowledge of GIS, public works, database design, and programming. The dedicated GIS staff shared and embraced this vision of a new interconnected GIS and made sure it came to fruition. ➢

Thousands of sewer and water asset records in Bellingham's maintenance management system are linked to a map location in the GIS.

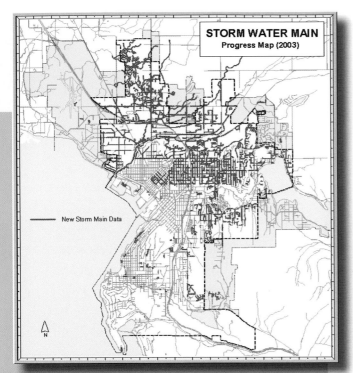

STORM WATER MAIN
Progress Map (2003)

—— New Storm Main Data

N

The city's successful development and management of the storm water utility is due in large part to the accurate and up-to-date relationships between the GIS and the assessors and the utility billing systems.

- Public Works Department's subdivision review and land subdivision records information and images
- Public Works Department's construction project tracking information and plan images
- Public Works Department's storm utility information system

In addition to the assessor, maintenance management, and utility billing data, all of the other data sets identified were internal to the Public Works Department. Staff used early versions of Microsoft Access to develop many of the city's stand-alone and legacy applications, particularly those developed to track and catalog subdivisions, construction, and development. The interface, data, and code had to be redesigned to use the data sets in the new interconnected system. The GIS staff redeveloped all of these systems into one fully relational data model with multiple relationships and data sharing throughout. Staffers rebuilt the input application interfaces around the new data model. Throughout the redesign process, they identified and created key fields to link these databases to each other and to different GIS data sets.

They also developed a series of update processes for each GIS data set and its related databases. For the maintenance management system, the information is directly joined to the associated GIS file. For the assessor's and utility billing systems, the Information Technology Services Department performs weekly imports of the desired data set into an Oracle data repository. All of the other GIS-integrated data

The following data sources were identified as being crucial to creating the data sets required for the new system:

- county assessor for property ownership, value, deed description, and land-use information
- maintenance management system for water and sewer structural and location information
- utility billing system for customer and service information

sets, such as the subdivision, survey, and construction plan lookup, use the same Oracle repository to store their data. The maintenance of mapping and interconnection of the numerous linked databases is a well-refined process. Staffers enter, map, and interconnect Bellingham's subdivision and development information within days of acceptance or approval.

Based on the new data model, the city's GIS staff released its first version of a Visual Basic® and MapObjects software-based customer service application in late 2001. GIS staff named the application CityIQ, short for City Information Query, and developed it around the premise of a one-stop information retrieval application that customers could use throughout the city. To date, more than a dozen separate data information systems with direct links to the GIS serve the public every day. The application is simple enough for the nontechnical user but dynamic enough to query and supply pertinent information. Customers now use more than sixty installations of the application. The range of users varies from customer service and utility workers to department heads and the mayor. The application provides quick and easy access to a range of integrated information.

Bellingham has experienced a number of benefits from the development of the interrelated data model. Its customer service staff can provide more information to customers in a quicker, more

efficient, and presentable manner. The city's successful development and management of the storm utility are due in large part to the accurate and up-to-date relationships between the GIS and the assessor's and utility billing systems. The city's GASB 34 asset reporting has worked well because of the interrelationship between the maintenance management, GIS, and construction project tracking applications. The Planning Department aggressively uses GIS for decision support in land-use management practices, impact analyses in development review, and modeling growth alternatives in long-range planning.

This complete data model vision continues to grow as Bellingham's user base expands and its interrelated data model develops. During the next few years, the city will build on its GIS investment with some challenging goals. With the staff members' extensive knowledge of database design, they will confidently tackle the next phase as they design geodatabase models for the land base and utility infrastructure. In 2004, Bellingham will release the second version of CityIQ, containing increased access to data relationships that have been continually developed. In 2004 or 2005, Internet and intranet development will expand beyond the current simple data download (*www.cob.org/pwgis*) to an ArcIMS site that takes advantage of the city's complete data model. ◉

Adapted from ESRI's *Water Writes,* Summer 2003, with permission from Don Burdick, GIS manager, city of Bellingham.

ADDITIONAL BENEFITS

Dozens of agencies work together to map shuttle debris

SECTOR *Public safety*
INDUSTRY *Government*

Ron Langhelm, Disaster Operations
Response/RISC, FEMA
www.fema.gov

Immediately following the *Columbia* space shuttle tragedy on February 1, 2003, dozens of agencies collaborated on the accident investigation. GIS provided the framework for these agencies to cooperate and track tens of thousands of debris pieces strewn across several states. While ESRI provided GIS software and professional services, dozens of institutions and agencies also used GIS tools daily.

Spearheaded by the National Aeronautics and Space Administration (NASA), Federal Emergency Management Agency (FEMA), U.S. Forest Service, Texas Forest Service, and U.S. Environmental Protection Agency (EPA), dozens of other agencies also came together hours after the disaster to begin the difficult job of piecing together clues that would help answer what happened and why.

FEMA established an information technology base at the Joint Information Center in Lufkin, Texas, using the Microsoft SQL Server™ database. This centralized command center served as the focal point for managing post-event data collection using ArcInfo, ArcSDE, and ArcIMS.

"We learned a lot from the events of New York City, and we knew that standardization was vital," said John J. Perry, chief of the Technical Services Branch/Emergency Support Function #5, FEMA. "We chose ESRI's ArcGIS 8.2 as our standard, and this helped tremendously because so many agencies were involved. We all used the same software and version. This cut down on confusion and streamlined our map production process."

The agencies set up emergency operation centers throughout Texas, Louisiana, and other states, each providing a localized data collection point. The centers began mapping debris quickly and through

hard work and cooperation established a standardized interconnected ArcGIS system.

Many other agencies and institutions volunteered their GIS services. Stephen F. Austin State University provided GIS mapping. "As soon as the event took place, we contacted the emergency center, and within a couple hours we were producing maps displaying where shuttle debris was located," said Susan Henderson, research associate at the university's Forest Resources Institute.

Under the EPA's direction, field-workers—volunteers, firefighters, law enforcement personnel, public safety officials, and department of transportation officials—collected debris and data and pinpointed locations using GPS. They brought the information to the command centers and analyzed it to predict possible locations of undiscovered debris. Central command orchestrated large-scale operational strategies and tactics after receiving map and tabular information uploads from each command

"As soon as the event took place, we contacted the emergency center, and within a couple hours we were producing maps displaying where shuttle debris was located."

—Susan Henderson

center. EPA also developed an ArcIMS intranet application that enabled users to create debris location maps.

EPA Region 6, in conjunction with Weston Solutions of West Chester, Pennsylvania, developed a mobile application for use in the shuttle debris recovery efforts. "This application was combined with components of ArcIMS and Microsoft .NET software for ease of use among the various agencies involved in the recovery effort," said Don Smith, Spill Prevention Control and Countermeasure Coordinator, EPA. "EPA personnel used HP iPAQ as the field instrument for collecting photo documentation, ➤

Staff from many agencies and volunteers collected debris and data pinpointing locations. This information was processed and analyzed in a GIS to predict possible locations of undiscovered debris.

GPS attributes, and item descriptions. The deployment of this combined application saved significant time and work-hours and reduced errors that are typical of similar paper-based systems."

Many different agencies used GIS not only for mapping debris but also for their independent responsibilities as well. NASA used the data for investigative purposes, EPA located potential health hazards such as toxic debris, and the U.S. Forest Service determined areas of thick forests to help allocate proper recovery resources.

The Texas Natural Resources Information System spurred major integration efforts. It input digital and paper map data, GPS data from various centers, and Microsoft Excel spreadsheets from Louisiana into the ArcSDE database, providing an enterprise environment for end users.

"The Texas Forest Service contacted us and asked us for some help," said Chris Williams, Database Administrator, Texas Natural Resources Information System. "We created a geodatabase layer in ArcSDE and established ArcGIS as the main mapping platform, and it just progressed from there. Several different entities built maps, but they all worked using the same GIS."   ⊙

ADDITIONAL BENEFITS

Powering Iceland's mission-critical emergency services

SECTOR *Public safety*
INDUSTRY *Government (International)*

Stefam Gudaugsson
GIS Manager, HNIT, Ltd.
www.hnit-baltic.lt/eng

The European Union is implementing a process to standardize the varying infrastructures among the countries within its organization. This will standardize all emergency response systems. The European Union voted to make all emergency response numbers 112. For Iceland this meant abandoning its disjointed network of independent agencies and reorganizing them so that one organizational body would handle all forms of emergency response. Iceland contracted privately held Neydarlinan HF to operate the country's entire emergency response system.

> *"Telephone operators responding to a 112 call in Iceland can now dispatch assistance from more than two hundred different response agencies nationwide."*

Shortly after its foundation, Neydarlinan approached HNIT, Ltd., a leading consulting firm in the field of GIS in Iceland, to develop an emergency response computer system that would include computer telephony, a relational database, GIS, and protocols for short messaging and pagers.

Telephone operators responding to a 112 call in Iceland can now dispatch assistance from more than two hundred different response agencies nationwide. They include fire, police, and ambulance units, and each has its own service area. Prior to the new system, each agency had separate emergency numbers.

In a typical scenario, an operator at Neydarlinan receives an incoming call. A telephone switch electronically identifies the caller's automatic identification number, which is matched in the Oracle database. The database provides the operator with the caller's address and postal code information, which is then georeferenced to locate the incident and determine the appropriate response agency. In moments, the operator has all the necessary information to dispatch a police, fire, medical, or ambulance unit.

"Our GIS has proven to be an extremely powerful solution for a mission-critical information system like the one at Neydarlinan," said Kristinn Gudmundsson, Project Manager at HNIT. "It enables the implementation of a fault-tolerant system with standard computing tools and opens up a new dimension in GIS." ⊙

In Iceland, emergency incidents are georeferenced to determine the location and appropriate agency to respond.

ADDITIONAL BENEFITS

Keeping the public informed helps crime prevention

SECTOR *Law enforcement/Criminal justice*
INDUSTRY *Government*

Thomas K. Casady
Chief of Police, City of Lincoln, Nebraska
www.ci.lincoln.ne.us; www.journalstar.com

The Lincoln Police Department (LPD) in Lincoln, Nebraska, is one of a handful of police agencies that makes available interactive, near-real-time crime mapping on the Internet. The department deployed an interactive Web mapping application in April 1999.

To protect the confidentiality of victims, the department edits all data fields except case number and date. The application includes links to more detailed information about interpreting maps and understanding geocoding. The LPD makes available extensive tabular data about significant police incidents at the neighborhood level. This application enables citizens to navigate to their own neighborhoods and view a detailed table of incidents within the past sixty days. Together, these applications are generating fifty- to sixty-thousand hits monthly on the department's Web site. Both applications employ scripts and routines that automate their daily update, requiring only occasional and minimal attention from staff.

Lincoln's daily newspaper, the *Lincoln Journal Star*, began publishing simplified police crime maps in 1999. The *Journal Star* presently publishes maps three times each week. These maps generate considerable public interest with their up-to-date informative content. Overall, Lincoln residents are more informed about the nature and extent of crime in the community because of GIS. Keeping the public well-informed energizes prevention strategies such as neighborhood watch, increases public support for law enforcement, and encourages tips and information from the public. ⊙

In Lincoln, Nebraska, the police department provides online information about significant police incidents at the neighborhood level.

ADDITIONAL BENEFITS

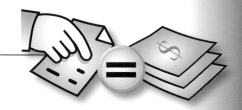

GENERATE REVENUE

The ever-present green ledger sheets are becoming things of the past in accounting offices as GIS technology becomes an integral part of financial planning, sales management, grant administration, and donation collection. For managing and generating revenue, GIS can't be beat. The technology gives financial and accounting managers an alternate way to view revenue and shows the geographic links between accounts and revenue streams.

Increasingly, financial managers are looking up from their spreadsheets and asking the question, "At what location is the revenue generated?" It is easy to see how geography enhances revenue management when you can see a link between a geographic area and successful revenue generation. Sales managers or fund-raisers can connect a specific demographic to the likelihood of either making a sale or securing a donation. These demographic profiles typically cluster in specific areas. Geographies such as tax rate areas, special tax districts, sales territories, or insurance rate zones often calculate fees for service.

Traditional financial management tools and software do a good job performing routine audits and analysis, but GIS can help enhance the analysis by answering spatially related questions. The answers can help identify revenues that might have slipped through the cracks. A GIS enables you to see where these "cracks" are, and enhanced revenue streams are a significant benefit of integrating GIS into traditional work flows.

Internet mapping technologies change the way a South Carolina county does business

SECTOR *Administration/Management*
INDUSTRY *Government*

Brian Fitzgerald
Richland County GIS, South Carolina
www.richlandmaps.com

In Richland County, South Carolina, Internet mapping has improved the county's internal business procedures and the way it serves its citizens. The countywide GIS program was designed for a broad base of users that includes GIS professionals, several data custodians, and many end users.

Richland County's customized Web interface, powered by ArcIMS and ArcSDE software from ESRI, provides county staff and the public with access to spatial information ranging from property values and hydrologic flow direction to aerial photographs and elevation contours. The technology has enabled the county to save time, make informed decisions, automate work flows, and provide the public with convenient access to local government information.

Located in central South Carolina and home to Columbia, the state capital and county seat, Richland County has a long history of progressive thinking. In 1786, responding to demands for an inland local government, South Carolina lawmakers packed up from Charleston and went looking for a more central meeting point. The town they founded, Columbia, marks the first instance in modern history when a functioning bureaucracy transferred its operations to a wilderness setting.

Business processes get better

Before the GIS implementation, many departments had relied on often inefficient and inaccurate paper-centric work flows. County staff had previously prepared soil evaluations for building permits by manually looking up tables in paper logs and referring to old paper maps to find a specific location. With few spatial references on the maps, finding a site was difficult at best. The new Internet mapping system with a digital orthophotography backdrop enables a permitting clerk to determine the soil, slope, and vegetation cover at the exact location of new construction in a matter of seconds, and even without extensive GIS training. As efficiency increased, the clerks could spend more time evaluating other aspects of the permitting process.

The county achieved similar results using GIS to determine flood insurance. Richland County once had to rely on paper flood-insurance rates published by the Federal Emergency Management Agency. Now, the GIS department maintains digital flood insurance rate maps in its spatial database and publishes them via ArcIMS to county employees and the public. In addition, users can refer to other data layers such as wetlands, ditches, surface flow accumulation, streams, and ponds. The county uses the new procedure to make more accurate flood zone determinations in less time. ➤

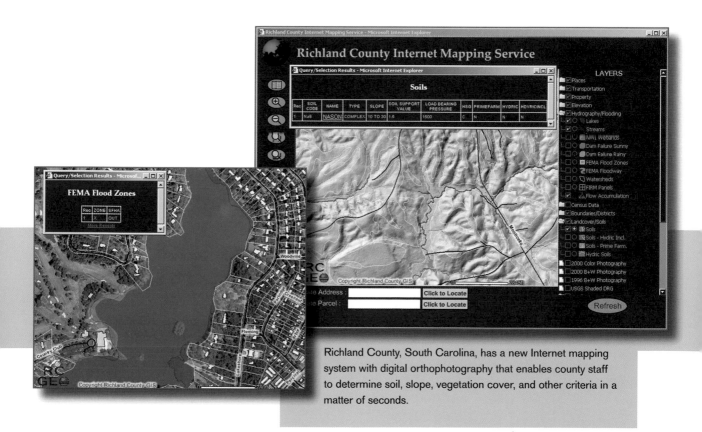

Richland County, South Carolina, has a new Internet mapping system with digital orthophotography that enables county staff to determine soil, slope, vegetation cover, and other criteria in a matter of seconds.

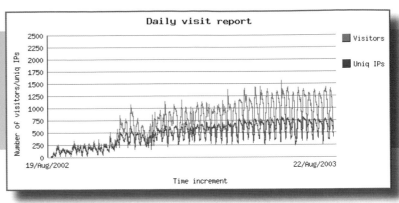

Richland County's Internet Mapping Service is popular with a variety of users including electric companies, engineers, surveyors, real estate brokers and many other departments and agencies.

Richland County also publishes elevation data in two-foot contours, hard and soft break lines, and digital terrain model points for all of its seven hundred square miles. This information supports the subdivision review and landscape planning analysis processes. The storm water manager and employees use GIS information daily to quickly browse surface runoff characteristics, elevation data, and impervious surfaces without having to spend additional time to complete in-depth analysis in a stormwater modeling environment. The convenience of viewing Richland County's GIS data from anywhere in the world in a matter of minutes provides excellent decision support, improves efficiency, and saves time and money.

The GIS Web tool has helped add several million dollars' worth of untaxed property to the tax roll.

Ensuring quality performance and recovering lost revenue

Richland County ensures the quality of its GIS data sets with devices that alert technicians to possible discrepancies. Online users can search for an address, and the system will automatically zoom to the area of interest using a geocoding service. However, when a user cannot locate the address entered, the search phrase is inserted into a database for later review by the addressing department. Approximately one in twenty search phrases result in an error and only 10 percent of these require changes to the data set. The Internet mapping application has verified the quality of Richland County's addressed street centerlines and provided an excellent data maintenance tool.

The Richland County assessor's office uses the mapping site extensively to perform re-assessments and view census data and property boundaries. By examining online aerial photography, staff can determine if a property should be considered agricultural or otherwise, eliminating the need to visit a parcel. The assessor's office uses the site to locate hunt clubs and other properties with dwellings that have eluded taxation. The GIS Web tool has helped add several million dollars' worth of untaxed property to the tax roll.

The treasurer's office uses the mapping application to locate mobile homes that haven't been taxed, and the planning department finds illegal dumpsites using online aerial photography. The sheriff's department uses the application to visualize search patterns for fugitives, print maps to take into the field, and determine areas of increased criminal activity. Hundreds of maps are printed every day to assist various departmental efforts that include going out into the field, posting zoning change notices and tax delinquent property signs, and reviewing permits.

Richland County also uses the ArcIMS application as part of a cost recovery and mitigation effort that involves the licensure of GIS data. Many data sets, including aerial photography, building footprints, street centerlines, and elevation data are available to the public in exchange for a licensing fee. Data is distributed for hundreds of tiles that are approximately one square mile in area. Developers, surveyors, real estate brokers, engineers, and architects place orders for GIS data via Richland County's online data ordering system, which uses ArcSDE and ArcIMS to display the tiling scheme and many of the data layers available for licensure. Users find their area of interest, select one or more tiles, and then generate an invoice by choosing data layers with a user-friendly interface similar to most online shopping sites. When an order is placed, all the pertinent information is stored in a database and an e-mail is sent to a staff member who fills the order and collects payment. In less than one year, this system has generated more than $50,000.

Richland County's Internet mapping service has been a great success with approximately one thousand unique visitors per day and more than fifty thousand hits per day. Users include electric companies, engineers, surveyors, real estate brokers, insurance companies, banks, and personnel from the natural resources, commerce, and transportation departments. Its extensive Internet mapping applications and its ease of use proves the service is an elegant solution to the social and technological barrier that exists between GIS professionals and the people who can benefit the most from it. ⊙

Department	Task	Benefit
Assessor's office	Locates hunt clubs and other properties with dwellings that previously weren't being taxed	Added several million dollars' worth of untaxed property to the tax roll since the program began
Treasurer's office	Uses the mapping application to locate mobile homes that have evaded taxes	
Licensure of GIS data—county's cost recovery program	Available to the public in exchange for a licensing fee	$50,000 generated in first twelve months—$87,000 up to July 2003

ADDITIONAL BENEFITS

County monitors false alarms, raises revenue, and reduces costs

SECTOR *Public safety*
INDUSTRY *Government*

Donald McGuire
Director of Emergency Services, Charles County, Maryland
www.charlescounty.org

Les Greenberg
CEO, AOT Public Safety Corporation
www.crywolf.us

In 1999 emergency service personnel in Charles County, Maryland, knew that the growing number of false alarms was affecting service delivery. Diverting law enforcement, fire, and emergency medical workers and resources from critical property and lifesaving activities cost time and money and placed personnel in risky situations that otherwise could have been avoided.

Less than an hour commute from Washington, D.C., historic Charles County has a population of 120,000 and is similar to a lot of other cities and counties across the country that are experiencing spiraling costs due to false-alarm responses. At the time, Charles County's alarm calls accounted for nearly 15 percent of all emergency calls for service, and nearly 98 percent of the alarm calls were false. A 10 percent annual increase in new alarm systems compounded the problem. At a weighted average cost of $225 to respond to a single emergency, the county estimated that it was spending more than $2.2 million a year to respond to approximately 9,800 alarms. That cost represented $18 in taxes for every person in the county.

Charles County developed a three-step plan to mitigate the problem. Like many jurisdictions, the county council first formulated and passed a strong false-alarm ordinance that defined the problem

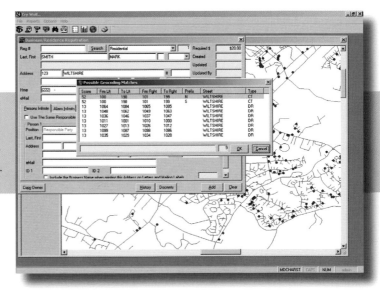

CryWolf, a GIS software, has relieved Charles County, Maryland, of performing many manual procedures by automatically tracking and billing alarm calls.

and established requirements to deal with it. The ordinance requires registration of all alarm systems in the county, subjects excessive false alarms to graduated fines, and ensures that citizens receive notice of all false alarms and due process through a formal appeals process. It also established a comprehensive program to educate the public about false alarms and describe ways to avoid them.

Next, the county established a False Alarm Reduction Unit (FARU) within the Department of Emergency Services to enforce the ordinance. In other jurisdictions, this responsibility has been successfully assigned to other departments such as police, sheriff, finance, or licensing. The key is to provide the public a central contact and focus the leadership necessary to combat the problem.

Charles County established procedures to implement the ordinance as its final step. Initially, it used manual procedures but soon found that the complexities involved in tracking false alarms, generating alarm notices, billing, managing receivables, and following hearings and appeals required an automated system. CryWolf software, designed by AOT Public Safety Corporation and powered by MapObjects software from ESRI, is specifically used for tracking and billing alarm calls. It helped relieve the burden of manual procedures in Charles County. Approximately forty cities, counties, and regions throughout the United States and Canada use the software, which generates revenue by invoicing fees and fines as well as reducing time and money spent on responding to false alarms.

Charles County soon began processing more than eight hundred false alarms per month with CryWolf software. The county's computer-aided dispatch system automatically transfers false-alarm data daily ➤

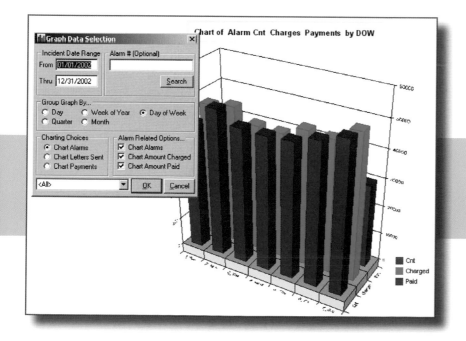

to CryWolf. It generates notices and invoices that are mailed to the alarm owners. This prompts owners of unregistered alarm systems to register immediately. The system also helps manage finances by aging receivables, highlighting slow payers, and generating late notices. Soon after installing the system, Donald P. McGuire, the county emergency services director, remarked, "With the CryWolf application, we've been able to accomplish more in four months than we were able to do in the preceding sixteen."

Within the first year, the number of false alarms fell, and registration and false-alarm fine revenue increased. Annual alarm company registrations soon more than doubled. During the next twelve months, alarm system registrations increased almost fivefold, registration and fine revenues dramatically increased to $250,000 annually, and CryWolf helped reduce false alarms in Charles County approximately 20 percent. At an average cost of $225, the county estimated it saved $300,000 per year in personnel and equipment costs.

If the 9,800 false alarms tracked by Charles County in fiscal year 2000 had continued to increase at their historic annual rate of 10 percent, the number of false alarms would have reached more than 13,000 during the 2003 fiscal year. Instead, actual false alarms were 6,815—nearly half those expected. The approximately 6,200 false alarms eliminated represent an annual savings in response costs greater than $1.3 million. This is in addition to the nearly $400,000 in registration fees and false-alarm fines that the county collected during the year.

With the new system, Charles County officials can devote more time to community education, crime prevention, heightened response time, and greater police presence. Alarm users better understand the impact of repeated false alarms and frequently inspect and update their systems.

According to McGuire, the implementation of the CryWolf application "has made FARU far more efficient and effective in reducing false alarms." He looks forward to its continued contribution to reducing the false-alarm rate in Charles County. ⊙

Estimated FY2003 cost without GIS	FY2003 cost with GIS	Annual response cost savings with GIS
13,000 alarms/year × $225 $2,925,000/year	6,815 alarms/year × $225 $1,533,375/year	Saved: 2,925,000 −1,533,375 $1,391,625

Plus revenue generated— registration fees and false-alarm fines.	$387,000/year (FY2003)—A 1,300 percent increase from FY1999.

Together, the cost savings and fee/fine revenue produced a total financial benefit of approximately $14.80 per county resident.

ADDITIONAL BENEFITS

Utah school trust fund receives its due

Utah has implemented a statewide GIS to help coordinate consistent geographic data acquisition and distribution. Utah developed its enterprise GIS solution at the broadest possible level, producing a

SECTOR *Economic development*
INDUSTRY *Government*
State of Utah
http://agrc.utah.gov

standardized, up-to-date, and comprehensive database. Utah maintains the State Geographic Information Database as an enterprise resource and structures the database to provide easy access to users and easy data loading for creators. All state agencies are involved through various executive branch requirements. Agencies participating at high levels include the Department of Natural Resources, the Department of Community and Economic Development, and the Department of Environmental Quality. Federal agencies more willingly share and enter into cooperative ventures because they can simultaneously reach nearly all affected players in the state.

This increased cooperation between federal and state agencies led to an important land exchange. The Utah School and Institutional Trust Lands Administration manages and collects fees for 3.2 million acres of surface lands and 4.7 million acres of mineral lands. The school fund receives more than 95 percent of the money collected. In 1999, 400,000 acres of federal and state lands were exchanged. As part of the swap, the state also received $200 million for the school trust fund. "Without good tools and data, this deal would not have happened," said Brad Barber, former deputy director of the Governor's Office of Planning and Budget, who helped negotiate the agreement. ⊙

The Utah trust fund achieved a high level of participation among all levels of government agencies.

Automated Geographic Reference Center

State
Tax Commission
Dept. Environmental Quality
State & Institutional Trust Land Adm.
Public Safety/Homeland Security
Natural Resources
Utah Geological Survey
Utah Olympic Public Security Command
Attorney Generals Office

Coordinating Groups
GIS Advisory Committee
Utah Geographic Information Council
Technical Interchange Group
Canyon Country Partnership
Utah Metadata Discussion
Utah Mapping Group
Utah Aerial Photography Consortium
Intermountain Hydro User Group
Colorado Plateau Data Committee
Uintah Basin Users Group

Federal
Bureau of Land Management
Forest Service
Park Service
Natural Resource Conservation Service
US Dept. of Transportation
US Geological Survey
Bureau of Census
Bureau of Indian Affairs

Local Government
Counties
Cities
Utah Assn. Counties
League of Cities & Towns
Association of Governments

Education
Higher Education
Utah Geographic Alliance
K-12

Tribal
Goshute Indian Tribe
Navajo Nation
Navajo Nation EPA
Northern Ute Indian Tribe
Northwestern Band of Shoshoni Nation
Paiute Indian Tribe of Utah
San Juan Southern Paiute Tribe
Skull Valley Band of Goshute Indians
White Mesa Ute Tribe

Please Note: These lists are not all inclusive.

Managing wilderness around a small community

SECTOR *Planning*
INDUSTRY *Government*

Dave Michaelson
Director of Long Range Planning and GIS
Gunnison County, Colorado
www.co.gunnison.co.us

Gunnison County, population fifteen thousand, is located on the western slopes of the Rocky Mountains in Colorado. In a beautiful setting at elevations ranging from 7,200 to 14,000 feet, 85 percent of Gunnison County is composed of federal lands and is home to four wilderness areas and a world-class ski resort.

Gunnison County faces many challenges including managing growth in a sensitive area with limited GIS and planning resources. "Gunnison County is a good example of how a small county has managed to transition from simple parcel mapping to an applied GIS methodology while still being able to provide the county's decision makers and the public with better information beyond just printing 'really cool maps,'" said Dave Michaelson, Gunnison County's director of long-range planning and GIS.

Initially, Michaelson developed partnerships with stakeholders in the Gunnison County Comprehensive Plan—Colorado Conservation Trust, the Sonoran Institute, Orton Family Foundation and CommunityViz, and The Nature Conservancy. He also outlined the county's expectations for a GIS and what would be necessary to reach that goal. The idea was to stay focused on the GIS objectives and not develop "data for data's sake."

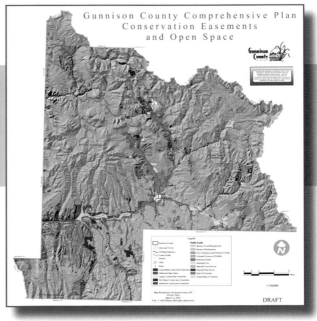

Gunnison County GIS has succeeded because it has demystified GIS and gained the trust of the decision makers and citizens it serves. The community accepts the technology as a critical tool to understand the implications of land-use decisions, not only in long-range planning but also in open space planning and environmental change in the context of an economy that depends primarily on summer and winter tourism.

GIS has increased revenue from map sales, according to Michaelson. He estimated the sale of beautiful GIS maps of hiking trails, wildlife

He estimated the sale of GIS maps of hiking trails, wildlife habitat, open space and other themes has covered up to 33 percent of the annual Gunnison County GIS budget.

habitat, open space, and other themes has covered up to 33 percent of the annual Gunnison County GIS budget. In addition, the county has created a program that provides customized maps to the business community. The county charges the client for staff time and map production. The program has exceeded expectations. ⊙

Gunnison County, Colorado, uses GIS as a planning tool and has developed an array of maps including an elevation profile, existing land use, conservation easements, and open space maps, the sales of which generate revenue for the county.

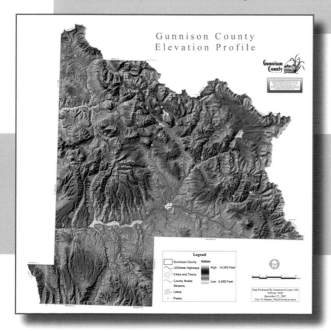

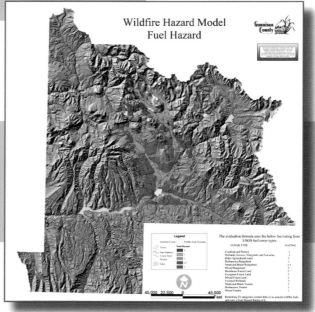

Vehicle fee collection raises revenue for Tennessee town

SECTOR *Administration/Management*
INDUSTRY *Government*

City of Bartlett, Tennessee
www.cityofbartlett.org

In Bartlett, Tennessee, GIS helps the city collect vehicle sticker fees. A review of the city budget showed that the $25 per vehicle sticker fee did not keep pace with the estimated number of households in Bartlett.

The county trustee's office had vehicles listed and located in unincorporated county areas instead of within the city limits. City staff used GIS to perform a simple address match against these addresses and identified a gap between county and city records that occurred when a revised annexation was not communicated and recorded properly.

Geocoding sixteen thousand additional records by ZIP Code yielded twenty-one hundred households that were not paying the required city vehicle sticker fee. The inclusion of these households will generate $52,500 annually in revenue for Bartlett. ⊙

The inclusion of these households will generate $52,500 annually in revenue for Bartlett.

ADDITIONAL BENEFITS

SUPPORT DECISION MAKING

Agencies, organizations, and businesses make hundreds of business decisions each day, which ultimately affect consumers, stockholders, taxpayers, businesses, and other stakeholders. While these choices often have immediate impacts, some have long lasting effects, which makes it all the more important to have the best information available to make the best possible decisions.

Skilled professionals rely on information technology tools to develop different solutions for delivering superior products and services. Managers and executives frequently seek out GIS as a way to support their ideas and proposals.

GIS is the optimal business decision support tool to improve the decision-making process or work flows because it is a computer-based technology capable of running multiple scenarios and options efficiently and rapidly. In a short period, GIS analyses can offer multiple alternatives for review by industry experts and management.

Traditional manual spreadsheet methods might extend a few analyses while a GIS approach can produce numerous graphic alternatives. GIS processing enables planners to review initial theories for feasibility before proposals are made. The ability of GIS to focus on geographic relationships in a problem provides a unique opportunity to incorporate data that traditionally would not be included for consideration in alternative decision processes. GIS helps businesses and government agencies make informed decisions and measure the impact of the decision's implementation. GIS technology also offers distinctive modeling and simulation tools that can be applied to "if-then" or "what-if" scenarios while taking advantage of its business intelligence and data warehousing, mining, and modeling capabilities. In addition, GIS is a visualization tool with no equal.

Baltimore CitiStat:
Mapping municipal accountability

SECTOR *Administration/Management*
INDUSTRY *Government*

Bill Ballard
Manager, Enterprise Services
Mayor's Office of Information Technology
City of Baltimore, Maryland
www.baltimorecity.gov

In fall 1999, Martin O'Malley was elected mayor of Baltimore. He inherited a city with chronic crime and grime problems that contributed to urban decay and population flight. Once a city of a million residents, the 2000 Census counted only 651,154 residents, 11.5 percent fewer than in 1990.

Determined to confront these problems, Mayor O'Malley looked to the successes of the New York Police Department's CompStat program, which is credited with significantly reducing crime in New York City. He enlisted the help of the late Jack Maple, former New York City deputy police commissioner and creator of the CompStat approach, to reverse the crime problems occurring in Baltimore. The CompStat process, which treats crime fighting as a business, is based on four tenets: accurate and timely intelligence, rapid deployment of resources, effective tactics and strategies, and relentless follow-up and assessment. These tenets encapsulate a common sense approach to crime fighting and have enabled Baltimore to achieve one of the largest major city crime reductions in the three years since its inception.

Prompted by the CompStat success in the police department, the mayor and Maple began to investigate the feasibility of a CompStat-like approach for Baltimore city government. The mayor was confident that Baltimore could implement and benefit from a comprehensive municipal management and accountability program. He named the initiative "CitiStat," and on June 29, 2000, CitiStat became a reality when the first real-time performance measurement and management accountability meeting was held in city hall. Since then, city agencies have held hundreds of CitiStat meetings. In CitiStat's first three years, the fiscal impact has exceeded $70,000,000 in savings from reduced overtime and operating costs and increased revenue streams. In addition to these financial benefits, the quality of city service delivery is also improving for city residents and businesses.

Getting back on track

One of America's great historic cities, Baltimore is a case study of a U.S. city in the process of industrialization, urbanization, immigration, and the generation of wealth and prosperity. The flight of city dwellers to the suburbs in search of bigger homes and safer streets has left some of the housing stock of a prior era empty and abandoned. The city that had fought and won a strategic battle against the British in the War of 1812 is now fighting a battle of urban survival.

Baltimore's location puts it at the center of a massive set of transportation networks—sea, air, rail,

Baltimore is one of the great historic cities in the United States.

and interstate highway. The Port of Baltimore, with its deep channel harbor, moves more than thirty million tons of goods that supply much of the East Coast and the Midwest. The Baltimore–Washington International Airport has become the busiest airport in the region, and the redeveloped Inner Harbor along with the National Aquarium and numerous historic sites attract more than seven million tourists to the city each year. Johns Hopkins University, a hospital and research center, is one of Baltimore's largest employers.

In 2000, the Baltimore city government employed approximately sixteen thousand people and managed a budget of $2 billion. The mayor faced an uninspired and demoralized workforce,

shrinking revenues, and growing expenses. Moreover, the mayor encountered additional challenges—an unhealthy economy, declining budgets, and unforeseen homeland defense expenditures. It was clear that the old way of doing business was not working.

Baltimore needed a way to break through the bureaucratic paralysis of the past and create a new process of managing government. Through CitiStat, Mayor O'Malley sought to "replace a culture of delay and avoidance with a culture of accountability and results monitored by technology that permeates every city agency." ➤

Process includes accountability

Before CitiStat, agency operations usually received reviews annually after budget approval. The CitiStat process reviews agency financial and operational issues and performance every two weeks. CitiStat meetings are mandatory and provide a two-way forum for open and honest discussion of issues and problem resolution. Meeting in the CitiStat room, decision makers can resolve an issue in minutes and avoid months of memos. "CitiStat changes what government does by measuring what it produces and creating a mechanism to make timely changes," O'Malley said. "If you can't measure it, you can't manage it."

Like the CompStat process, CitiStat helps agencies focus on performing their fundamental mission and managing their primary goals and objectives. The mayor said, "City government should not try to be all things to all people but, instead, should do a few things well such as fight crime and grime, provide opportunities for kids, and create an environment that welcomes private investment."

In advance of their CitiStat meeting with the mayor, agencies must submit an operational performance matrix, which is a standardized reporting template. The CitiStat team consists of analysts and technicians who organize, analyze, and, in some cases, investigate the validity of the data. They geocode, map, and compare agency complaints and other location-based information with agency geographic management areas.

They prepare charts, graphs, and maps of the information showing past performance, status, and emerging trends. CitiStat analysts also produce an executive briefing memorandum for the CitiStat panel and assist in identifying topics of interest for the meeting. These documents provide not only a summary of the information within the CitiStat reports but also data abnormalities, problem areas, and suggestions for agency initiatives. In these instances the CitiStat analyst for the particular agency has performed research on best practices, met with agency members, and looked at past reporting periods before recommending new methods. After the meeting, the CityStat team sends a concise and focused follow-up memo to the agency detailing issues, requests for additional information, and actions to be taken prior to the next meeting.

The CitiStat room provides an intimate and effective setting for dialogue between panelists and agency managers. It also accommodates a large seating area for agency staff and visitors. Spreadsheets, charts, graphs, and maps detailing agency performance are projected onto two large screens. Additional audio and video capabilities enable the full range of multimedia content. From a control room, CitiStat technical analysts prepare and present meeting material from multiple computer systems for display on the two screens.

Accurate data for intelligent decisions

Obtaining accurate and timely intelligence is the first and most critical step of the CitiStat process. Technical analysts collect an array of data regarding agency activities and performance that includes personnel information about overtime, sick time, and leave time. They track agency projects and review scope, schedules, and cost. Much of the rest of the data relates to the agency's performance of service delivery and response to complaints. Because this is geographic data, it is geocoded and integrated with existing geographic information for analysis and display. Analysts perform geographic density analyses on incident and complaint data. For example, they determine the occurrence of drug-related crimes in proximity to schools or vacant and abandoned buildings. This method helped identify hot spot areas in Baltimore for complaints such as crime, dirty alleys, dirty lots, and illegal dumping on public and private property.

CitiStat focuses on cross-discipline or cross-agency analysis where it can develop a comprehensive view of available agency information. When done well, this process can optimize synergy and maximize the benefits of other agencies and their information. Maple applied this principle to fighting crime by removing neighborhood trash and fixing broken streetlights. Even if an agency manages and analyzes its own operational information well, it is seldom combined with other agency data for additional analysis. This is where geographic information, technology, and related analysis prove invaluable. Mapping the number of missed trash pickup complaints for a specific area might suggest a problem with a supervisor, while mapping potholes can help recommend which roads are candidates for reconstruction.

Collecting geographic information and mapping everything from potholes to homicides is an essential and effective part of the CitiStat process and meeting dialogue. One by-product of CitiStat was the creation of an enterprise geographic information services group within the Mayor's Office of Information Technology. The group formed because of the following reasons:

The CitiStat room is equipped to accommodate agency staff and has a range of multimedia capabilities.

- Most city information is geographic in nature and its location is meaningful.
- Maps and location-based analysis communicate quickly and clearly to a broad audience.
- An assortment of geographic information can be integrated on one canvas and relationships between seemingly disparate geographic data sets can be observed.
- The single, common geography of the city points toward the need for a centrally managed and shared geographic data warehouse.
- Investments in geographic data and technology demand maximum value.
- Without a citywide managing entity, redundancies would occur across agencies.

The benefits of sharing data

The CitiStat process has had an enormous impact on the sharing of information across agencies. This applies to all data, but especially to the shared use of geographic information. Only a few years ago, some ➢

agencies were making maps on the photocopying machines and pasting them together. They now have access to detailed geographic basemap data and are developing their own geographic data layers that, in turn, will be made available to all. The shared use of geographic information has put traditional data into a meaningful context that helps illustrate patterns, suggest strategies, and enable economies.

The CitiTrack system and Baltimore's new 311 "One Call Center" has been a critical addition to the CitiStat accountability tool. CitiTrack is an enterprise-wide application that manages the intake, routing, and resolution of service requests. City residents can report a nonemergency problem or complaint by either calling 311 or by online entry through the Baltimore Web site. Call takers triage the nature of calls into one of three hundred possible city service types and obtain the incident location information. The caller receives a customer service request tracking number for follow-up. Call takers route the service request address and type to the appropriate city agency for resolution. The city completes and closes the service request after resolving the issue.

To prepare for CitiStat meetings, the CitiTrack system offers a variety of reports and analyses on new, closed, and overdue service requests; average time open, and average time to close. In addition, the address-based service requests are geocoded and mapped. Problems or patterns become immediately evident when they are produced on a map and combined with agency management areas. The CitiTrack system commonly displays maps during CitiStat meetings to substantiate an issue in real time.

The CitiTrack system observes overtime and service request trends and measures the effects of new tactics. Mayor O'Malley said, "With our 311 One Call Center on the front end and CitiStat on the back end, we are making consistent and measurable progress toward identifying and resolving problems in a timely and cost-effective manner." The success of Baltimore's

Baltimore's GIS has helped solve crimes by providing accurate and timely intelligence, rapid deployment of resources, and effective strategies.

CitiTrack and 311 One Call Center earned it the 2003 Customer Relationship Management Excellence Award in the Large Enterprise Category by Gartner, Inc., a leading research firm helping clients benefit from technology.

The CitiTrack database consists of spatial data files generated via the geographic street network layer, part of the city's enterprise geographic information warehouse. Agency geographic management areas are coded onto the street network layer and translated into the CitiTrack database. This enables staff to identify responsible agency management areas after a constituent call and service request address are matched to a CitiTrack street segment record. Staff can then route the service request to the appropriate supervisor for resolution.

As CitiStat permeates all of Baltimore city government, individual agencies have established their own "Stat" processes for their internal operations resulting in PoliceStat; FireStat; DPWStat; HousingStat; and issue-focused "Stat" processes such as ProjectStat, DrugStat, and KidStat. In this way, all managers and all employees become accountable, and their efforts are measured in a consistent manner.

Since the development of the CitiStat program in Baltimore, visitors from around the United States and other countries have attended CitiStat sessions to learn more about the program and begin their own implementations. In addition, Mayor O'Malley brings his message to other places. On October 14, 2003, Mayor O'Malley spoke at a conference in London attended by British officials, including Prime Minister Tony Blair, to show how cities such as London and Liverpool could benefit from a CitiStat application for fighting crime.

Like the CompStat process that has become ubiquitous in crime-fighting organizations, the simplicity and benefits of the CitiStat process are becoming widely recognized. CitiStat works because it spawns accountability. As Mayor O'Malley stated, "That is CitiStat. It is how we run city government in Baltimore." ⊙

ADDITIONAL BENEFITS

Missouri agriculture ensures food safety

SECTOR *Agriculture*
INDUSTRY *Natural resources*

Ryan Lanclos
Program Coordinator
State of Missouri Homeland Security GIS
www.mda.state.mo.us

Time seems to stand still in the middle of an American farm field, but agriculture is changing as rapidly as any other aspect of the contemporary world.

Recent events have made the American agricultural industry keenly aware of the need for precautions to safeguard the nation's food supply. The foot-and-mouth disease outbreak in Europe and the terrorist attacks of September 11, 2001, have made the United States realize that foreign animal disease outbreaks or terrorist attacks could endanger its crops and livestock.

… first responders can relay an accurate assessment of a situation back to their office.

State and federal agencies are implementing homeland security measures to protect resources and consumers. Farmers are monitoring activities more closely to prevent a catastrophic event that could endanger agricultural resources and cripple an already struggling economy. Although most homeland security efforts focus on terrorist activity, animal disease outbreaks are not limited to deliberate acts of bioterrorism and can occur naturally.

To help safeguard the state's agricultural industry and food supply, the Missouri Department of

Agriculture is implementing a plan that uses GIS to help monitor, model, and deal with any agriculturally related event. Contingency modeling for potential foreign animal disease outbreaks is a driving force in the implementation of an enterprise GIS for the department.

The Exotic Newcastle Disease Map Book is an example of one GIS application already in place. It instantly provides first responders with critical information to handle a disease outbreak. Using ArcGIS software from ESRI, the system produces detailed maps about confirmed animal feeding operations for poultry throughout the state. By providing a basemap for each feeding operation location in the state, the map book offers information about the county, individual sites, areas surrounding each feeding operation, road networks that provide access to each site, and any water bodies near a site that could be contaminated. The system also delineates one-, two-, and three-kilometer containment areas around each site.

Using hard-copy maps produced by the map book, digital maps published with the ArcGIS Publisher extension, and handheld GPS units in the field, first responders can relay an accurate assessment of a situation back to their office. This seamless flow of accurate data minimizes lag time, a critical factor in first responder situations, and enables officials to make effective decisions.

From these assessments and subsequent testing, the state veterinarian can determine an appropriate response that includes the preferred method for disease eradication. Based on this protocol, GIS provides department staff with information that aids them in selecting methods for cleansing the site with minimal environmental impact.

GIS helps the Missouri Department of Agriculture respond more efficiently to foreign animal disease situations in the state. Giving the department's users a comprehensive view of a site's local conditions, as well as information on the surrounding area, provides enhanced decision support for rapid initial needs assessments. These assessments include determining the number of personnel needed for quarantine control and traffic monitoring; estimating the animal population located in proximity to the affected area, which also determines the manpower needed for subsequent quarantine control and disease eradication; and establishing the size of decontamination areas around an infected site.

Agriculture is inherently spatial in nature and well positioned for the integration of GIS. Quickly providing maps to field personnel has decreased response time and improved the decision-making process. ArcGIS provides the Missouri Department of Agriculture with a powerful analytical tool that helps the department adapt to a changing world and assist in the state's homeland security efforts. ⊙

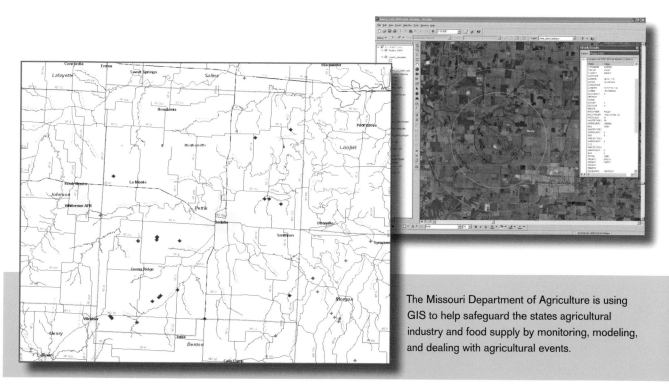

The Missouri Department of Agriculture is using GIS to help safeguard the states agricultural industry and food supply by monitoring, modeling, and dealing with agricultural events.

Easing county redistricting pains

SECTOR *Elections*
INDUSTRY *Government*

Tim Johnson
GIS Programmer/Analyst and GIS Manager
Maricopa County, Arizona
www.maricopa.gov

The Maricopa County, Arizona, Recorder/ Elections Department's mission is to provide access to the electoral process for citizens, jurisdictions, candidates, the legislature, and special interest groups so that they have equal access and may readily participate in elections.

State law requires Maricopa County to redraw its district and precinct lines frequently to adjust for population growth and court caseload. Redistricting and reprecincting must also follow traditional principles, such as respecting "communities of interest," using recognizable physical features as boundaries and remaining compact and contiguous. State law specifies timelines and other requirements, and because Arizona is under the jurisdiction of the Voting Rights Act, the U.S. Department of Justice must analyze and approve all changes to elections boundaries. Nevertheless, many concerned citizens feel that redistricting is done behind closed doors by people who have only their own interests at heart.

To meet the demands of redistricting, the Maricopa County Recorder/Elections Department developed its On-Line Redistricting System, a Web-based application that enables review of, comment on, and analysis of various redistricting scenarios for proposed district maps. The ArcIMS Internet application helps to provide open redistricting, ease of use, rapid updating, and flexibility in how users can view and analyze plans.

Maricopa County also elected to build and deploy an extension of the On-Line Redistricting System that is available to any interested citizen or group. The system enables them to create and modify their own redistricting plans. It mimics much of the functionality of expensive stand-alone redistricting software programs but is available at no cost to citizens.

The community can participate in the redistricting process with the On-Line Redistricting System. ⊙

Maricopa County's On-Line Redistricting System is a Web-based application with tools for reviewing and analyzing various redistricting scenarios.

ADDITIONAL BENEFITS

Deregulated utility companies seek competitive advantage

Deregulation in the utility industry forced many companies to become more competitive and increase their marketing and public relations practices. With more competition, utility companies now must create brand awareness and win customer loyalty but continue to be cost-efficient. Deregulation has made utility companies more aware of business costs. These costs are becoming extraordinarily visible, and utility companies are looking for ways to operate more efficiently. Reliant Energy of Houston uses GIS to make better decisions about which steps to take.

SECTOR *Electric and gas*
INDUSTRY *Utilities*

Jeff Myerson
Reliant Energy
www.reliant.com

Utilities constantly seek ways to increase customer retention, notify customers about new products or service changes, improve customer service, and optimize services and delivery. ArcView Business Analyst has helped Reliant Energy develop targeted direct-mail campaigns, notify customers of changes, build brand recognition, improve customer service by optimizing service center sites within a certain drive-time to most of its customers, locate new service centers based on the number of customers, and identify outdoor advertising opportunities.

Jeff Myerson, manager of GIS at Reliant Energy said, "Having access to nationwide data sets of business listings, demographics, street, and consumer information all in one GIS application is key to assisting utility companies to make better business decisions during this time of deregulation." ⊙

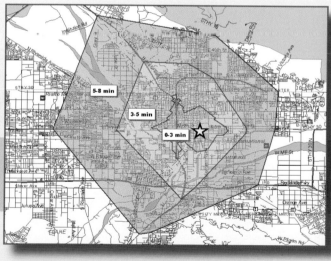

Reliant Energy of Houston uses GIS to optimize service to its customers. Customized maps show drive times to service centers.

ADDITIONAL BENEFITS

Tracking wildland fires

SECTOR *Public safety*
INDUSTRY *Government*

Zeke Lunder
GIS Coordinator, NorthTree Fire International
www.northtreefire.com

In October 2003, fires raged across Southern California in San Diego, San Bernardino, Los Angeles, Ventura, and Riverside counties. Flames scorched hundreds of thousands of acres, displaced tens of thousands of people, and destroyed thousands of homes. As emergency responders worked mightily to put out the fires, computer mapping played a key role in many areas.

GIS provided three-dimensional maps of fire areas and communities and incident perimeter maps. It helped identify critical facilities and allocate resources and equipment. Emergency personnel used GIS to analyze vegetation, slope, and other landscape features to understand potential and actual fire behavior. Public information professionals relied on GIS to respond to media inquiries about fire locations, road closures, and damaged or undamaged property sites. Law enforcement used GIS to plan evacuations and monitor events while government officials drew on Internet mapping and other GIS services to understand wildfire damage and communicate information to constituents and other agencies. GIS also played a role in daily strategy and assessment meetings, providing mitigation plans and decision support.

Strategic planning on the fly

In San Diego County, the human-caused Cedar Fire started near the mountain town of Ramona and spread rapidly, fueled by acres of dry brush and fanned by strong Santa Ana winds. It consumed more than 140,000 acres in its first day. Containment came ten days later, only after the flames burned 273,246 acres, destroyed 2,232 homes, and killed fourteen people. Keeping six thousand firefighters appraised of the speed and ferocity of the blaze proved to be a massive undertaking.

As the Cedar Fire grew, the California Department of Forestry and Fire Protection (CDF) contacted NorthTree Fire International, a fire response GIS contractor based in Monterey, California. Successful fire operations depend on obtaining accurate information about the location of the fire quickly, establishing priorities, and implementing a response plan—activities that benefit from GIS. Outfitted

The Cedar Fire consumed more than 273,000 acres in San Diego County, California. It was one of many fires that raged throughout Southern California in October 2003.

with a plotter, numerous PCs, and an array of ESRI's software, the contractor's GIS trailer and staff journeyed to San Diego to support the CDF GIS team members. The trailer became a round-the-clock nerve center, providing firefighters and decision makers with accurate and up-to-date maps.

With ArcView, ArcInfo Workstation, ArcGrid™, ArcGIS 3D Analyst™, ArcGIS Spatial Analyst, ArcScene™, ArcPress™, Adobe® Illustrator®, Adobe Photoshop®, and Adobe Acrobat® softwares, GIS team members produced hundreds of detailed maps, integrating multiple information sources from field observations to infrared helicopter data.

"The most critical maps we generated were those for the morning briefings, and they had to be done on time," says Colby Barr, GIS mapping specialist for NorthTree Fire International." There is no way you tell thousands of firefighters, 'I'm sorry I don't have the information you need.' These maps are a necessity. They use them to be aware of their surroundings and the larger context of the fire to strategize for the day."

At the morning briefings, firefighters received full-size plots depicting the fire progression, active or contained fire areas, bulldozer lines, and other critical data such as supply drop points and water sources. These maps detailed each section of the fire line and which division was responsible for it. In addition, division group supervisors, branch directors, and strike team leaders received detailed eleven- by seventeen-inch map packets. These sheets, which firefighters used to chart their daily assignments, showed roads, buildings, water sources, drop points, and staging areas.

Creating numerous informational resources for the fire's incident command, GIS team members

NorthTree Fire, International provided a GIS trailer and staff to support the firefighting efforts on the Cedar Fire.

enabled decision makers to effectively allocate hand crews, bulldozers, engines, aircraft, and other assets. "If we didn't have these maps, the firefighters wouldn't have known where to go, how to get there, or what their assignments were," said Jeff Harter, situation unit leader, CDF. "Using GIS we could pull all of the necessary information and help them make their plans of attack. It is amazing how much a difference it makes to have good quality maps that are easy to understand and tell a story." ⊙

Calculating catastrophic losses

SECTOR *Banking and insurance*
INDUSTRY *Business*

Rick Thomas
Head of Research, PartnerRe, Ltd.
www.partnerre.com

Based in Bermuda, Partner Reinsurance Company, Ltd. (PartnerRe), an international reinsurance group and an intelligent provider of risk assumption products for the global insurance and capital markets, has embedded GIS analysis tools into PartnerRe's enterprisewide GIS system, PRECED. The system is based on ESRI's ArcSDE and Oracle and enables underwriters to access information from their desktops about global natural hazards and expected loss levels.

> *"The company made a strategic decision … GIS was essential to that decision, and history has proved so far that we made the right decision."* —Rick Thomas

According to Rick Thomas, head of research at PartnerRe in Switzerland, "The company made a strategic decision to model natural catastrophes. GIS was essential to that decision, and history has proved so far that we made the right decision."

Thomas leads a team of scientists that develops and supports catastrophe modeling tools. Using GIS, the group has created global pricing tools for hurricanes and earthquakes, an accumulation control and exposure recording system for the group, and modeling tools to calculate group exposure to catastrophic perils. The team quantifies PartnerRe group exposure to catastrophes such as tornados, earthquakes, floods, hurricanes, and other natural hazards. The underwriting team then has the tools to calculate the correct premiums for catastrophe exposure.

PartnerRe created its own system because no globally applicable off-the-shelf tools measured the geographic accumulation of exposure or offered the necessary flexibility. The penalty for mistakes in accumulation control is frequently bankruptcy, which makes accuracy paramount. As an added benefit, PartnerRe's detailed accumulation control can deploy more capital than its competitors at the same level of confidence.

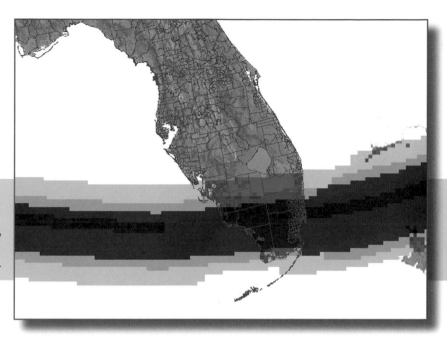

PartnerRe uses GIS to model natural catastrophes such as tornados, earthquakes, floods, and hurricanes to determine risk factors.

According to Thomas, "Geography determines the link between natural hazards and our clients' exposures. ESRI has enabled us to preserve this natural link in the IT systems we use to monitor the risks we bear. Our models are key elements in the calculations we do to estimate and allocate our capital costs." ⊙

"Geography determines the link between the natural hazards and our clients' exposure."

Rick Thomas

ADDITIONAL BENEFITS

Developing smart growth scenarios

SECTOR *Planning*
INDUSTRY *Government (International)*

Christopher J. Pettit
Department of Geospatial Science
RMIT University—Melbourne
www.rmit.edu.au

The shire (township) of Hervey Bay is situated along the east coast of Australia and includes North Fraser Island, designated a world heritage area by the World Heritage Commission for the United Nations Educational, Scientific, and Cultural Organization. Like many coastal townships along the east coast of Australia, Hervey Bay is experiencing strong population growth. Within the last decade the shire's population doubled to more than forty-four thousand and is expected to nearly double again by 2021.

The final scenario created for Hervey Bay focused on the principle of sustainable development, incorporated areas of both environmental and economic significance, and allowed trade-offs to occur between these sometimes conflicting concerns.

Together, the Australian Research Council, the Queensland Department of Local Government and Planning, and the Hervey Bay City Council developed a sustainable development-based land-use scenario for the shire using ArcGIS and a GIS-based planning support system called What if? from What If, Inc., of Hudson, Ohio.

ArcGIS manages the various data sets and enters them into What if?, enabling the Hervey Bay City Council Integrated Planning Unit to quickly begin running and testing various planning scenarios based on numerous user-specified indicators. The formulation of each of the draft planning scenarios required the council planners to specify which suitability factors would affect the future allocation of specific land uses. What if? presented the planners with an intuitive and easy-to-use graphical user interface that generated alternative land-use scenarios on the fly.

The final scenario created for Hervey Bay focused on the principle of sustainable development, incorporated areas of both environmental and economic significance, and allowed trade-offs to occur between these sometimes conflicting concerns. The Hervey Bay City Council Integrated Planning Unit developed the final set of suitability factor weightings and ratings to generate the digitally developed future land-use strategy. The unit overlaid the existing boundary to analyze the existing land capacity of the city with respect to the projected land-use location allocations for 2021. The results show that the existing city boundary needs to be extended to accommodate the projected increase in low-density residential and park-residential land-use categories.

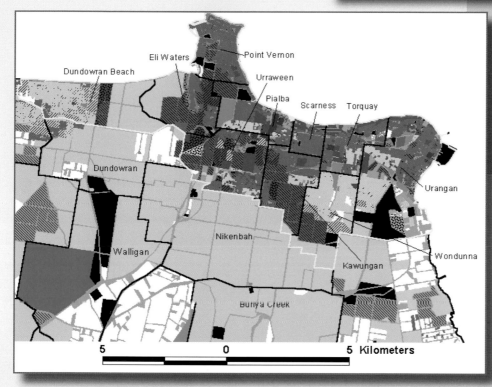

Dundowran Beach

Eli Waters

Point Vernon

Urraween

Pialba

Scarness   Torquay

Dundowran

Urangan

Nikenbah

Walligan

Wondunna

Kawungan

Bunya Creek

5   0   5 Kilometers

Hervey Bay's
GIS-based planning
support system
helps planners
quickly run and test
planning scenarios
based on user
specified criteria.

In rural and coastal local government areas in Australia, strategic plans are updated and published approximately every five to six years. Traditionally, these plans have been laboriously formulated through the use of expert knowledge and visual interpretation of paper map outputs and tabular information. Tools such as ArcGIS and What if? easily produce alternative scenarios they can test, recreate, and present to council members and the community for feedback. This greatly improves the decision-making process. ⊙

Providing safety and protecting rights in Southern California

SECTOR *Planning*
INDUSTRY *Government*

Mike Heslin
GIS Coordinator, City of Moreno Valley, California
www.ci.moreno-valley.ca.us

The city of Moreno Valley, located in Southern California halfway between Los Angeles and Palm Springs, wanted to decide where adult businesses could locate within city limits. The city acted in response to a court case in a neighboring city that did not have an adult-oriented business ordinance. Moreno Valley used its extensive GIS to research and outline suitable areas for these businesses. To preserve the health and safety of the community, the city also used GIS to define sensitive areas where adult businesses could not operate. The GIS team worked closely with city planners and city attorneys to develop the adult business use ordinance.

1 **Moreno Valley zoning map**

By mapping existing conditions, city planners can quickly and efficiently assemble the spatial/attribute layers, including land use and zoning, needed to conduct the study. GIS enables the city to define land-use and zoning activities and establish criteria to allow adult business activities within city limits including a predefined distance from sensitive areas.

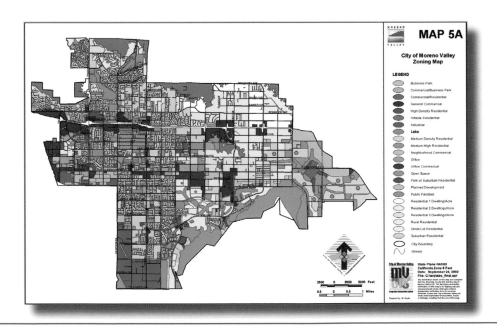

2 **Classify the data**

Based on categories of interest, the city divided the zoning map into four zones, including commercial, industrial, sensitive areas, and not available for adult businesses.

3 **Additional reclassification**

The city overlaid the sensitive areas on the results of step 2. These areas include existing and proposed schools, day care centers, group facilities, churches, and parks. Existing sexually oriented businesses were also mapped.

4 **Combined overlays**

All sensitive and restricted areas listed were merged into one map, resulting in 20,069 acres of sensitive areas, 1,372 acres of industrial area, 3,524 acres of commercial area, and 5,807 acres not available for adult business.

5 **Buffer analysis**

A five-hundred-foot buffer is applied to all restrictive/sensitive areas, and a one-thousand-foot buffer is applied to existing adult businesses. The city will not consider parcels within the buffered areas for possible adult business designation.

6 **Refining the spatial analysis**

Moreno Valley parcels are overlaid to determine existing parcels that can be included in the designated adult business zoning district.

7 **Overlay and query analysis**

GIS analysis reveals 568 parcels that meet the adult business ordinance criteria. GIS highlights these parcels in yellow. ➢

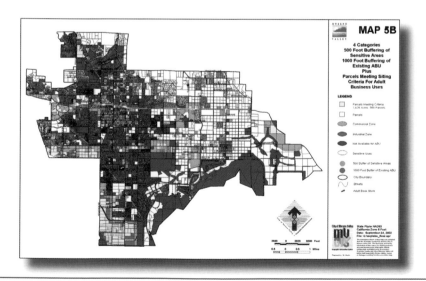

8 **Refining the spatial analysis within commercial/industrial sites**

Commercial/industrial parcels meeting adult business use criteria are symbolized to reflect their respective existing zoning.

Additional steps:

Identifying vacant parcels that meet criteria with a structure value equal to $0 may further refine the adult business use study. Furthermore, a report on adult business use can be generated for all parcels selected (meeting criteria). The report includes parcel count, assessor's parcel number, zone, acreage, land value, structure value, flag, street address, owner name, acreage in commercial, acreage in industrial, parcel count of parcels with a $0 structure value, and total acreage of sites meeting criteria.

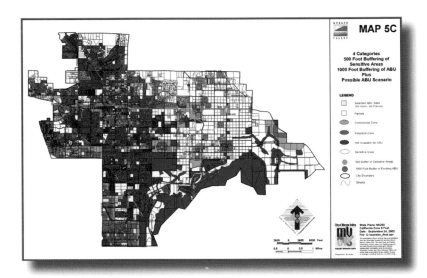

One more additional analysis capability:

The city generated possible adult business use scenarios. One scenario placed an adult business, generated a one-thousand-foot buffer, and placed another adult business, and so on. These scenarios revealed forty possible adult business use sites in acres.

This is a typical GIS decision support process in which a data rich GIS can help planners submit proposals to the decision-making bodies, taking into account all proposed use criteria required. ☉

ADDITIONAL BENEFITS

Initiative greens urban spaces

The Trust for Public Land (TPL) is a private, non-profit land conservation organization dedicated to improving the quality of life in cities and rural areas. Founded in 1972, TPL specializes in the practice of conservation real estate—applying its expertise in planning, negotiation, public finance, and real estate law to advance the organization's mission of "conserving land for people." It has helped conserve more than 1.6 million acres with a fair market value of nearly $3 billion.

To ensure that the organization's work focuses on one of its priorities—developing parks in central city neighborhoods—TPL launched a national GIS initiative known as "Greenprinting GIS" in 2001. This multidimensional strategic planning initiative involves a diverse mix of mapping, decision support, and community building services to help identify the need as well as service the demand for new parks and open space in low-income, densely populated neighborhoods. For the sustained success of the Greenprinting GIS program, TPL has forged alliances with Earth Analytic of Santa Fe, New Mexico, and CommunityViz and Computer Terrain Modeling, both of Boulder, Colorado, which enhance the capabilities of TPL's small in-house GIS team.

With GIS, TPL can assemble a variety of demographic and physiographic data sets to create clear and compelling maps that illustrate the extent and distribution of community parkland resources. TPL's Greenprinting GIS work is particularly sensitive to

SECTOR Planning
INDUSTRY Not for profit
Ted Harrison
Senior Vice President of National Programs
The Trust for Public Land
www.tpl.org

the needs of poor children, targeting neighborhoods with high concentrations of children and poverty as priority sites for creating new parks.

GIS has provided TPL with a way to constantly improve its Greenprinting process and dramatically decrease the amount of time it takes to complete a Greenprinting study for a city.

Using the storytelling capabilities of GIS, TPL and its local partners can more efficiently target land acquisition opportunities and solicit financing and community support for new green spaces and public gathering places. In addition, GIS has provided TPL with a way to constantly improve its Greenprinting process and dramatically decrease the amount of time it takes to complete a Greenprinting study for a city. The first study, done in Los Angeles, took seven months to complete. Recent studies in New York, Boston, and Charlotte, North Carolina, have ➤

The Trust for Public Land Greenprinting initiative uses mapping decision support and community building techniques to identify needs and service the demand for new parks and open space in low-income, densely populated areas.

taken less than two months. This helps to speed up and facilitate the decision-making process and expand the number of communities and landscapes that TPL can productively serve. ⊙

AID BUDGETING

As widespread financial belt-tightening causes many fiscal planners to sharpen their pencils, GIS is helping to bring the spreadsheet into focus. With its analytical, reporting, and tracking functions, GIS is a natural "geospreadsheet."

In general, the budget process attempts to match revenues with anticipated costs. Managers planning their budgets can apply GIS to processes such as fiscal impact analysis, economic feasibility studies, grant justification and verification, reimbursements, and estimating allocations related to ongoing operations.

Traditional accounting practices tie revenues and expenditures to specific activities or customer numbers. Using GIS during budgeting suggests that expenditures of staffing, equipment, property management, and most business operations are spatially related or connected to specific locations. Likewise, any organization, company, or agency can use GIS to understand where its revenue is coming from. By linking revenues and expenditures to geography, GIS is an exceptional tool for preparing a detailed cost analysis.

While most financial and accounting professionals expect to see budgets in the form of rows and columns, they can perform their budget analyses more efficiently by looking at the geographies or territories assigned to the revenues and expenditures.

Midwest town boosts financial standing

SECTOR *Finance*
INDUSTRY *Government*

Todd Jackson
GIS Manager, City of Westerville, Ohio
www.ci.westerville.oh.us

Westerville, Ohio, sprouted up at a crossroad in central Ohio in the early nineteenth century. Nearly two centuries later, it's a fast-growing suburb of Columbus, and its city government is on a technology fast track that's streamlining and maximizing service delivery.

An enterprise GIS is directly responsible for much of the city's progress in revamping business procedures and slashing work-hours required for tasks. Like most cities, Westerville initially invested in a GIS to replace time-consuming, manual map production methods. The city's use of GIS has grown extensively since its implementation in 1995. The system now benefits ten city departments. Among its many uses, the GIS helps the police analyze crime, supports utilities management, and sustains the planning department. City staff can access GIS data via the city's intranet, and the public can gather spatial information with the click of a mouse at Westerville's Internet site.

A request from the city manager and finance director for property information for two primary investor services gave the GIS department the opportunity to highlight the value of GIS. A primary investor provides a service to people or institutions that invest in public agencies by rating the agency's risk factor.

The GIS queried and analyzed the property data including total city area, percent of land use, zoning, and undeveloped and exempt property. Based on this information, the system generated a report and map that were part of an information package that went to the two primary investor services with a request for a bond rating upgrade.

Many factors determine a municipal bond rating, including the public agency's economy, debt structure, financial condition, demographics, and

PROPERTY DETAILS

Parcel ID	31734202002000
Zoning	PCC
Property Name	Pointe at Polaris
Property Owner	Continental Realty
Owner Location	150 E. Broad Street, Columbus, OH 43215
Location	State Route 3/Polaris Parkway
Description	2nd floor office, multi-tenant, new construction, multiple units available
Size	4,900 sf
Price	None
Term of Lease	5 year
Availability	Immediate
Status	Available
Company Name	Continental Real Estate
Realestate Agent	Mark Catalano
Contact Person	Mark Catalano
Phone Number	(614) 883-1069
Email Contact	mcatalano@continental-realestate.com

management practices. In Westerville's case, four different city divisions in three departments compile this data.

"With the GIS we were able to access all the requested information and provide additional data to support the findings in ninety minutes," said Westerville's GIS manager, Todd Jackson. "Some of the data we generated was the percent of undeveloped land throughout the city. Though the investor services requested only the percent undeveloped, we felt it was important to indicate that the majority of the undeveloped land was zoned commercial and ready for development. We also pointed out that the city had previously invested financial resources to provide the utilities and infrastructure needed to service and access these undeveloped areas, which made the land development-ready and less of a liability."

> *"With the GIS we were able to access all the requested information and provide additional data to support the findings in ninety minutes." —Todd Jackson*

The end result was good news for Westerville. It received a bond rating upgrade. The comprehensive reports and supporting materials generated by the GIS, along with the city's reputation for paying back loans and strong fiscal practices, contributed to the positive decision. The new bond rating has helped reduce the city's interest rate 1.27 percent, giving its citizens a savings of more than $1 million over twenty years. ➤

The Westerville GIS department was able to provide property information to two primary investor services, which helped the city receive a bond rating upgrade.

Old interest rate	
Principal balance	$6,500,000.00
Interest rate	5.50%
Payments per year	12
Monthly payment	$44,712.68
Years	20
Total interest paid	$4,231,042.00

New interest rate	
Principal balance	$6,500,000.00
Interest rate	4.23%
Payments per year	12
Monthly payment	$40,180.93
Years	20
Total interest paid	$3,143,423.97

Benefit description	Calculated value (where appropriate)
• A savings of 25 percent in interest paid over the length of the loan. What does this mean? It means lower taxes for city and township homeowners.	Based on a twenty-year loan with an interest rate of 4.23 percent, Westerville taxpayers will save $1,087,618.03, which equates to a 25 percent savings compared to the original interest rate derived from the previous bond rating.
"We borrowed the funds at a very attractive rate," said Jack Winkel, Westerville finance director, "which means that the voters will pay less than the 0.24 mill* that they approved."	The savings is calculated by subtracting the interest to be paid using the new interest rate from the interest to be paid using the old interest rate and amortizing each rate over twenty years, the length of the loan.
Though he is not yet certain how much the drop in millage** will be, Winkel estimated it to be adjusted downward to 0.2 mill for Westerville residents.	$4,231,042.00 −3,143,423.97 $1,087,618.03

* A mill is defined as 1/10 of 1 percent and is multiplied by the assessed value after any exemptions have been subtracted to calculate the taxes.
** Millage is the percentage of value that is used in calculating taxes.

TOTAL SAVINGS	$1,087,618.03

"This is one example that dispels the myth that GIS is only a mapmaking tool. Finance and accounting are usually not included on the list of the top five or ten departments using GIS, but they should be," said Jackson. "Upper management is conscientious about every dollar spent and continuously looking for new ways to save money." GIS has enabled Westerville to appropriately account for existing land use and infrastructure, and this will influence future external investment in the city. ⊙

"Finance and accounting are usually not included on the list of the top five or ten departments using GIS, but they should be."

Todd Jackson

ADDITIONAL BENEFITS

Asset management is a breeze

In 1999, the Governmental Accounting Standards Board (GASB) adopted sweeping changes that sent many state and local governments scrambling. GASB sets accounting and financial reporting rules for all U.S. state and local governments. Its function is important because financial reporting gives the public a clear picture of a state or local government's fiscal standing and is the basis for investment, credit, and many regulatory decisions.

GASB's drastic changes showed up in Statement 34, which fundamentally departed from the current reporting model and required accounting of public domain infrastructure fixed assets. Compliance with GASB 34 guaranteed longer and more complex government financial statements that would be more difficult to prepare and audit, especially during conversion to the new model.

Meeting the challenge

In eastern Maine, the city of Saco has distinguished itself as one of the first communities to meet GASB 34 requirements and ensure its strong bond rating. Saco uses its GASB 34 implementation as an opportunity to show how the benefits of GIS reach throughout the organization.

The city's finance department worked with public works to create a plan that included the development of a GIS-based asset management system to improve the city's financial position through GASB 34. The system forged better relationships among departments and provided the foundation for a citywide GIS to increase operational efficiency and improve service delivery.

SECTOR *Finance*
INDUSTRY *Government*

Lisa Parker
Finance Director, City of Saco, Maine
www.sacomaine.org/departments/finance/gasb34.shtml

The team designed the plan to take advantage of the ability of GIS to enhance the city's asset inventory, improve fiscal planning, track and convey costs and benefits yielded from investments, facilitate conveyance of information to citizens and elected officials, support interdepartmental collaboration and resource sharing, and aid in the budgeting process.

Saco fully complied with GASB 34 requirements for the fiscal year ending June 30, 2001, finishing a year ahead of the first required deadline. Long-range planning, which emphasized long-term operations, accurate asset mapping, and maintenance has paid off. One of the most notable ancillary benefits of the system has been improved working relationships with elected officials. Before Saco could proceed with its GIS and GASB 34 plans, the city had to secure permission for the project. Finance and public works staffers met several times with city council members to explain the mandate, outline the plan's benefits, and gain approval for the technology investments.

A broad-reaching plan

The city's asset management solution had four phases: data collection, system implementation, training, and documentation of results. ➢

Fortunately, Saco had already conducted a combined sewer overflow inventory for approximately 70 percent of the total sewer system infrastructure. The city also surveyed pavement condition. Saco collected existing infrastructure asset information in the field using GPS units for location information and inspection surveys for asset condition information. Workers input the data in handheld computers.

Rather than develop the asset management system, the city subcontracted with an outside vendor to complete this phase of the work. Staff training and compilation of results proved essential in documenting the city's return on investment.

Shortly after its GASB 34 implementation, two national agencies upgraded Saco's bond rating. The bond upgrades saved Saco twenty basis points when the city issued a school improvement bond, amounting to $2 million in savings to citizens over twenty years and enabling greater flexibility in the budgeting process.

Saco's efforts laid the foundation for a citywide GIS, supported a new partnership between the finance and public works departments, and assisted in the preparation of a federal grant application.

Saco has earned national and state recognition for its management excellence, garnering accolades such as

- the National Government Finance Officers Association (GFOA) Certificate of Achievement for Excellence in Financial Reporting for the city's GASB 34 compliant comprehensive annual financial report for the fiscal year ending June 30, 2001,
- the GFOA Distinguished Budget Presentation Award for the fiscal year ending June 30, 2002, and
- the Margaret Chase Smith Maine State Quality Award in recognition of leadership, strategic planning, and quality improvement. ⊙

ADDITIONAL BENEFITS

Keeping track of utility pole attachments

CenterPoint Energy, a large U.S. natural gas and electric distribution company, uses a GIS application to manage utility pole attachments from cable television and communications companies. The company uses the GIS database to track the communication attachments in many ways. It easily generates text or map format for reports of attachments by area, owner, and type. It merges legal text and map images to produce a legal contract document that shows specific poles leased to a communication company within the area on the map. The GIS data also produces pole counts and generates lease attachment billings. The GIS helps CenterPoint manage approximately $4 million in annual revenue. ⊙

SECTOR *Electric and gas*
INDUSTRY *Utilities*
CenterPoint Energy
www.centerpointenergy.com

ADDITIONAL BENEFITS

Planning for the future

SECTOR *Planning*
INDUSTRY *Government*
Washoe County, Nevada
www.co.washoe.nv.us

You can use GIS to help plan what a place will be like in the future. That gives a community the time it needs to provide housing, facilities, and other services. Planners at Washoe County, Nevada, use GIS to help create twenty-year plans for areas within the county.

What they do…

1 **Forecast future growth**

Based on how population has grown in the past, planners predict how it will grow in each area over the next twenty years.

2 **Map what's already there**

They use GIS to create maps showing the existing population, the land use, and street network. They also map which undeveloped areas are suitable for future growth.

3 **Develop the plan**

Using the GIS-generated maps, planners work with community groups to make sure enough land is set aside for the housing and other services needed to support the projected population growth over the next twenty years. They use GIS to create maps showing where the new housing and other services should be built and to calculate how much land is allocated to the different types of housing.

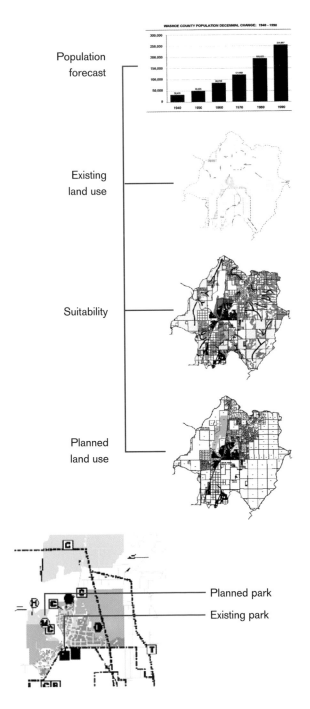

4 Put the plan into practice

The various agencies that provide the services (police, schools, and libraries) use GIS to create maps of each phase of the plan as it develops—which parks are built and which are still planned and locations of water and sewer lines.

5 Make revisions

As population forecasts and the needs of the community change, the community groups and the planners use GIS to make changes to the plan and create revised maps and figures.

How GIS helps make the plan...

- Information from a variety of maps and data-bases can be combined in the GIS and displayed on one map or on a series of them.
- The GIS lets you combine data to create new information about a place. For example, you can combine digital maps of soils, slopes, and land cover to find areas suitable for building (areas having suitable soils, on a gradual slope, and not on a wetland).

- Since all edits are made on the computer, it's easy to map several different scenarios or make changes to the maps. When you're ready, you can print as many copies of the maps as you need right from the GIS.

More examples of using GIS to plan for the future...

- The William S. Hart Union High School District in Santa Clarita, California, uses GIS to help forecast student enrollment seven years into the future. They collect and analyze demographic and development data for each neighborhood. That tells them where and when they will need to build new schools.
- A private consulting firm used GIS to help develop a master plan for the City of Kuwait by integrating information on population, con-struction, and employment. The plan will help the city tackle long-term development issues, as well as provide a guide for day-to-day decisions such as evaluating building permits.

ADDITIONAL BENEFITS

California town uses GIS to apply for grants

SECTOR *Public safety*
INDUSTRY *Government*

Nancy Bradshaw
City of Hemet, California
www.ci.hemet.ca.us

The fire department in Hemet, California, needed specific emergency response data to apply for a grant that would pay for lifesaving equipment. The process of mapping historical incident response data showed an increase in call volume due to a larger jurisdiction, which the city attributed to new housing projects and annexations. The GIS helped Hemet acquire a $22,450 grant from the California State Office of Transportation Safety to purchase a Hurst Jaws of Life tool, which improves service in the growing community. ⊙

ADDITIONAL BENEFITS

AUTOMATE WORK FLOW

From a management perspective, GIS generates widespread benefits efficiently and productively. Linked to business processes, GIS offers an organization the opportunity to automate a variety of tasks that expedite work flows and enhance an organization's ability to react efficiently during a crisis.

Managers can find opportunities to automate with GIS via system integration in enterprise resource planning, mobile workforce automation, e-business activities, and customer relationship management systems. Managers can use GIS to automate routine analysis, map production, data creation and maintenance, reporting, and statistical analysis. Often, geoprocessing can yield significant reductions in task replication. Mobile GIS can reduce the number of trips to the office for data retrieval, and it offers a data collection avenue to eliminate steps between the field and traditional key entry. Internet-based solutions can cross reference data repositories and deliver a self-help approach to perform many tasks that traditionally require direct personnel involvement. GIS can automate repetitive tasks seamlessly so that nontechnical staff can maximize productivity while not feeling intimidated by the software. Many GIS applications are readily available to organizations out of the box or as solutions from third-party developers.

GIS operates on a reusable data foundation that interacts and supports numerous business systems and information bases. This data reuse and reassignment of the information to different problems is unique to GIS technology because GIS can communicate with back- and front-office systems and access real-time data and information. Grounded in geography, GIS offers an exceptional method for performing business processes, unlike traditional data organization methodologies.

Spatially enabling public information and analysis

SECTOR *Health and human services*
INDUSTRY *Government*

Jared Shoultz, MA
Manager, Informatics Section

Murray B. Hudson, MPH
Director, Office of Public Health Statistics and Information Services
South Carolina Department of Health and Environmental Control
www.scdhec.gov

State public health agencies deal with many health issues every day. Each topic requires agencies to process, integrate, analyze, and distribute massive amounts of spatial and attribute data to many different end users with a range of technical capabilities and diverse needs. With limited resources, state public health agencies must determine the most appropriate way to access and use spatial and statistical data to facilitate the decision-making process for public health assessment and surveillance. This requires addressing several variables including time and budget constraints, agency cooperation and collaboration, enterprise architecture, legacy processes, privacy concerns, and existing infrastructure.

The South Carolina Department of Health and Environmental Control (SC DHEC) has been using GIS technology to help deal with these issues, and it has experienced a substantial return on its initial investment on GIS software, staff, processes, and data. SC DHEC is a large state agency employing more than six thousand employees. It is charged with promoting and protecting the health of the public and the environment. The agency is organized to serve the public under four broad areas: environmental quality control, health services, health regulations, and ocean and coastal resource management. Many of the agency's divisions have their own GIS staff.

Within the agency's Public Health Statistics and Information Services (PHSIS) program area, the Division of Biostatistics and Health GIS serves as a model for the benefits of automating daily activities

The South Carolina Assessment Network is a Web-based system. Users go through a multistep process to select a unit of analysis that includes demographic variables, such as race, sex, ethnicity, education level, and spatial and temporal variables such as year, ZIP Code, county, and health district.

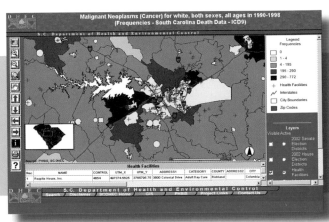

with GIS. Framing public health issues in a spatial context enhances services, promotes inter- and extra-agency cooperation, and dramatically reduces response time to pressing questions about the analysis of public health data.

A one-stop shop

The Division of Biostatistics and Health GIS has employed a diverse set of ESRI's software to automate, integrate, and apply public health data. The GIS has helped PHSIS achieve its mission to provide the right information to the right people in the right time and format. The GIS accomplishes this with interactive map services, linked relational database management systems, and a strict set of data quality assurance and quality control measures.

The division uses ArcIMS, ArcSDE, ArcGIS, and various ESRI extensions including RouteServer IMS, ArcGIS StreetMap™, ArcGIS Spatial Analyst, and Network Analyst coupled with programming languages and relational database management systems to power its enterprise GIS. This suite of technology enables staff to keep GIS layers

accessible, current, and well documented—a process that had been handled with hand-drawn paper maps. Previously, it was almost impossible to study health problems at a scale below county boundaries without expending a tremendous amount of time and energy. Now with the automated approach, staff can complete these studies in a timely and efficient manner.

The Division of Biostatistics and Health GIS began using GIS more than thirteen years ago after PHSIS received a grant to fund the Vital Records Geographic Referencing System project, a three-year demonstration project in GIS to test the feasibility of geocoding births and deaths.

The GIS program has evolved over time and taken advantage of technological advances including the movement toward commercial off-the-shelf software and relational database management systems. Streamlined and cost-effective internal applications have freed up resources for other projects and given an agency with a limited budget the ability to accomplish its mission in a more ➤

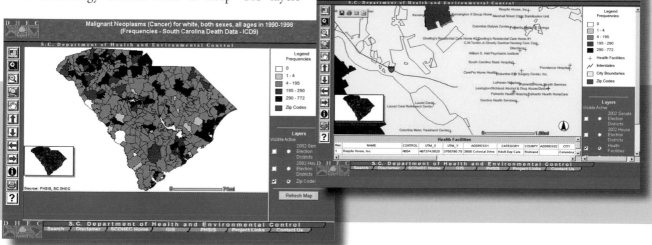

transparent manner. The Division of Biostatistics recently changed its name to the Division of Biostatistics and Health GIS to reflect the growing importance of this technology in its daily activities. This unit has grown from a one-person shop to a team that serves as the support center for all public health GIS issues in South Carolina.

Streamlined and cost-effective internal applications have freed up resources for other projects and given an agency with a limited budget the ability to accomplish its mission in a more transparent manner.

Streamlining work flows

Birth certificates, death certificates, and various state registries provide vital record information. Users process this information to standardize addresses and the record-level content for use in different forms of analysis. Much of this analysis is strictly statistical, but users must georeference and geocode this information for spatial analysis. The process creates a file that can be de-identified with a variety of methods to ensure patient confidentiality and adherence to various regulations. The resulting file is integrated into the GIS for analyses ranging from point-level density analysis to state-level trend analysis. This gives a variety of users access to different scales of this data cluster, network distance, spatial–temporal analyses, and simple overlays.

Users can overlay environmental, demographic, utilities, political boundaries, public health boundaries, public health infrastructure, and other data onto georeferenced patient data. The technology can draw out relationships and serve as a preliminary assessment tool that identifies trends, disparities, and possible correlations that may warrant further investigation. This process would have been difficult to accomplish by hand, but with the automated GIS process, users can analyze relationships with only a few clicks of a mouse.

The geocoding process at SC DHEC has gone from a strictly in-house procedure to a hybrid process that sends addresses to a commercial organization for geocoding. The addresses are returned to SC DHEC with an acceptable match rate. The agency then interactively matches the records to increase the overall match rate. Matching can be done at a variety of different geographic levels including exact address; street-level; and ZIP Code, county, and state centroid. An ongoing initiative, the Vital Records Reengineering project, will create an inline/online geocoding tool, accessible only to SC DHEC employees and enabling geocoding and address verification at the point of data entry. This will increase the accuracy of current public health data sets and enable access to the spatial components of this data in a timelier manner.

The Division of Biostatistics and Health GIS has traditionally responded to requests for statistics and maps with an intensive manual process, which often did not adequately stress the spatial component of the issue in question. Automating the process with GIS technology and the Internet has cut response times dramatically, provided a decision support tool for public health, and assisted with mandates in the area of public health surveillance and assessment. With automated systems, such as the South Carolina Assessment Network (SCAN), end users can customize their requests and modify them interactively while freeing up staff hours to focus on in-depth issues and analysis in public health. With systems such as SCAN, SC DHEC is now serving a wider audience and implementing different levels of access to applications and data based on the end user and intended use for the data.

The Internet advantage

SCAN is a Web-based system that gives users the ability to go through a multistep process of selecting a unit of analysis that includes demographic variables such as race, sex, ethnicity, education level, marital status, and age and spatial and temporal variables such as year, ZIP Code, county, and health district. Users can apply these factors to public health questions such as birth characteristics, causes of death, health indicators, and pregnancy outcomes. Users can generate many different types of statistical and graphical output including interactive tables, maps, bar charts, and trend lines with frequencies and varied forms of rates. By putting this system online, end users have real-time access to information they need.

Other automated systems include the Emergency Shelters application, which tracks official hurricane shelters and their vital attributes including capacity, current evacuees, and current status. The sheltering system provides a variety of different end-user reports based on different geographic and organizational requirements. Emergency management agencies, first responders, and affected individuals can use this Web-based service. By embedding GIS into this application, SC DHEC can give driving directions to every shelter; geographic visualization and verification; and spatial analysis of shelter locations, accessibility, and efficiency. This tool is a model for a dual-use system used by a variety of different state agencies and the public. It conserves limited resources and promotes agency cooperation and collaboration. ⊙

"GIS has provided an exponential return on investment for our agency by automating our work flow and freeing up staff time to focus on more in-depth health analysis, while giving our end users real-time access to vital public health information."

Jared Shoultz

ADDITIONAL BENEFITS

Better service with integrated land records

SECTOR *Cadastral*
INDUSTRY *Government (International)*
Sheila Glanfield, City of Oshawa, Ontario, Canada
Nancy Kemp, City of Oshawa, Ontario, Canada
Gary Waters, President, NovaLIS Technologies
www.novalistech.org

In 1999, the city of Oshawa, Ontario, Canada, began exploring ways to replace its various existing land-records systems with one integrated process that could share land-related information across the city's departments. The city wanted to update data one time instead of having to duplicate the work in different departments.

Located on the shore of Lake Ontario, about thirty miles east of downtown Toronto, Oshawa has a population of approximately 142,000 people and is the dominant economic center for the provincial region.

> *"We feel like GIS is now part of our core business processes and not just an interesting technology used by a select few. We take great pride in the success we have achieved."*
>
> *—Sheila Glanfield*

At the time, the city's existing database operated on a VAX system inaccessible to most city staff and difficult to use. Since 1991, staff had been using customized ArcInfo and ArcView for editing graphic layers and as a map-enabled land information system, but they wanted to expand the system to include land processes such as permits, site plans, and complaints.

Oshawa chose the Land Development Office, Assessment Office, Parcel Editor, and GATE solutions from NovaLIS Technologies. Combined with ArcInfo and ArcView software, these products enabled the city to integrate its land-records information, place mapping information, and supply it to the desktop. In addition to streamlining business processes, the new system helped the city provide better service to residents, businesses, and visitors as well as take care of Y2K compliance issues.

The project merged separate systems—a land information database, development tracking applications, and a GIS—into one integrated process tailored to meet the specific business requirements of the city.

In August 2000, the new integrated system went live. The city trained more than one hundred staff members, and many employees with no prior GIS experience successfully adopted the system. "For us, it was key that the new system be easy to use and give everyone involved in processing applications access to the information they needed to do their job on their desktop," said Sheila Glanfield, business analyst for Oshawa. "We feel like GIS is now part of our core business processes and not just an interesting technology used by a select few. We take great pride in the success we have achieved."

The new software has enabled the city to automate the work flow for application review, approval,

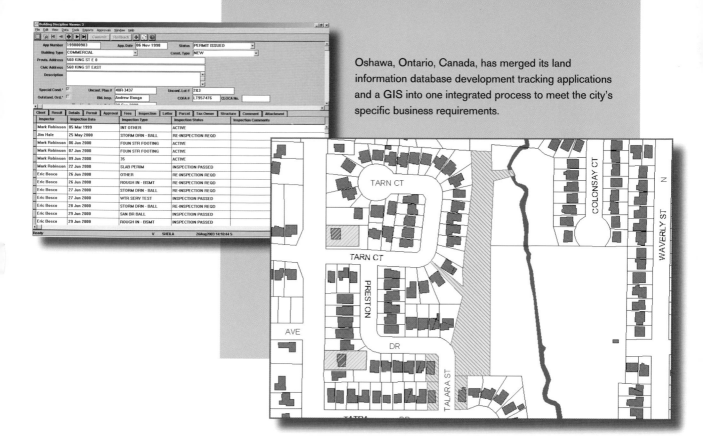

Oshawa, Ontario, Canada, has merged its land information database development tracking applications and a GIS into one integrated process to meet the city's specific business requirements.

inspection, and map updates. Users can now immediately view and analyze the most up-to-date map information along with reference information such as hazardous and environmental conditions. Built-in quality control measures ensure that all requirements are met and that tasks are carried out in the correct order.

The city will incorporate subdivisions, minor variances, and official plan amendments into the Oshawa land information system once departments complete their review. "We re-engineered our business processes so that information has to be entered only once and then can be used by all of the other departments," said Nancy Kemp, business analyst for Oshawa. "We can also track and evaluate efficiency to monitor and improve our business processes."

Instead of gathering information from eight different data sources to determine if a property complies with the city's zoning regulations, inspectors now access all spatial and attribute information about a particular property in one location. This saves the city time and money and, more importantly, improves customer service. ⊙

ADDITIONAL BENEFITS

Hawaii Office of Elections debuts interactive Web site

SECTOR Elections
INDUSTRY Government

David Rosenbrock
Data Processing Coordinator, Hawaii Office of Elections
www.state.hi.us/elections

In 2002, the state of Hawaii launched an ArcIMS Web site to provide up-to-date, accurate election information to Hawaiians. The Web site, *www.state.hi.us/elections*, informs voters about polling locations and other election issues. "We wanted to give voters a heads up that they might not be voting at the same place they have been for the past ten years," said David Rosenbrock, data processing coordinator for Hawaii's Office of Elections Computer Support Department.

According to Rosenbrock, the state has 292 designated polling locations, 51 districts, and 104 different ballot types. Hawaii is required to provide ballots in English, Japanese, Chinese, and Ilocano. The 2002 election cycle included 51 state house seats; 25 senate seats; 9 city council seats on Oahu; and county council seats on Maui, Kauai, and the island of Hawaii. In addition, Maui and Kauai had mayoral contests. The ballots also included county charter issues and constitutional amendments.

"The ballot can be so complex that it helps if people have an idea of what to expect before they arrive at the polls," said Rosenbrock. "We are trying to lessen confusion for voters before they get to their polling places. Anything we can do to provide information to the public and make the registration and voting process easier is a great benefit to everyone in the state."

Before the 2002 election, Hawaii's Office of Elections (OE) employed ESRI's Professional Services Group to help build the site. Together, they implemented a Web site where viewers can search for information including their district and precinct numbers, assigned polling places, and maps to these locations. Users can also preview ballots specific to their precinct before election day. This Web site was built using a modified version of the sample Active Server Pages code that comes with ArcIMS.

The site offers voters an alternative to calling or visiting OE for this information. In 2002, redistricting affected about one third of the state's registered voters, meaning nearly 180,000 voters found themselves in new districts or assigned to new polling locations. For these reasons, it was important to make the data available in an easy-to-access format for Hawaii's primary, general, and special elections that year.

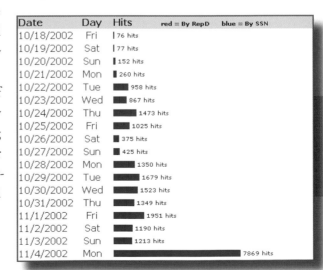

Hawaii's elections Web site gives viewers the opportunity to search for information in one of two ways—by district/precinct number or by the last six digits of their social security number. Rosenbrock explained that registered voters are sent a yellow card identifying their polling place and district/precinct number. When users select the latter option, the application searches approximately 600,000 registered voter records in a Microsoft Access database to find all voters whose last six digits match. Voters can select their address from the returned choices. Then they can opt to view a map of their polling location, see a report of their polling site and precinct number, or preview their ballot. The mapping option displays a map showing streets and then zooms to the assigned polling location. More than half of the hits are searches using a social security number.

The Internet site receives more than ten thousand hits a day as election day nears.

One important feature lets voters choose from one of four languages to view ballots in an easy-to-read format. "Additionally, GIS enables citizens to query their voter status at times convenient to them and not only during OE's working hours," said Rosenbrock. "GIS gave OE a responsible balance of costs of service to service provided."

The Internet site receives more than ten thousand hits a day as election day nears. "Most of the feedback we have received has been positive," said Rosenbrock. "The Web site will remain a part of OE services and will be refined and improved." He added that local schools have been using the site as an educational tool in the classroom. ⊙

美國眾議員 空席补選 二零零三年任期為滿 只限投一人			
○	(N) ANAND, Kabba	○	(R) MARUMOTO, Barbara C.
○	(R) ANDERSON, Whitney T.	○	(N) MATAAFA, Sophie
○	(D) BRITOS, Paul	○	(D) MATSUNAGA, Matt
○	(R) CARROLL, John (Mahina)	○	(R) McDERMOTT, Bob
○	(D) CASE, Ed	○	(N) MCNETT, Mark

Hawaii's ArcIMS Web site provides accurate election information including ballots in four languages, polling locations, and other election topics.

Polling Place			English	Chinese	Ilocano	Japanese
Hauula Elem Sch	view map	view report	ballot	ballot	ballot	ballot
Kahaluu Elem Sch	view map	view report	ballot	ballot	ballot	ballot
Kahaluu Elem Sch	view map	view report	ballot	ballot	ballot	ballot
Heeia Elem Sch	view map	view report	ballot	ballot	ballot	ballot
Windward Community College	view map	view report	ballot	ballot	ballot	ballot
Ahuimanu Elem Sch	view map	view report	ballot	ballot	ballot	ballot

new search

ADDITIONAL BENEFITS

Enforcing safety on the rails

SECTOR *Transportation systems and networks*
INDUSTRY *Transportation*

Boris Nejkovsky
Chief Engineer, ENSCO Rail Division
www.ensco.com

In 2001, Amtrak launched the Acela Express, a high-speed train serving the Washington, D.C./New York–Boston corridor. This is the first high-speed rail service available in the United States. With the addition of this service, Federal Railroad Administration (FRA) officials established new regulations that require daily monitoring of vertical and lateral accelerations (i.e., the quality of ride) of rail vehicles traveling at speeds in excess of 150 mph.

Data typically reaches the communications service in less than two minutes.

When the agency developed the regulation, collecting information this way was expensive and consumed valuable time. Someone had to physically remove the ride quality data collection files at the end of a trip and post-process the information to determine if any rough riding areas existed. Amtrak decided to automate the process with the help of an FRA-sponsored research and development project that remotely monitors the quality of rides and automatically transmits the information via wireless links to a central database and GIS. ENSCO, Inc,

of Springfield, Virginia, developed the Remote Monitor System. It consists of four main components: data collection units, a wireless communications link, a relational database management system, and ArcView and the reporting system.

Two data collection units are currently installed onboard six Acela trains. The units consist of a computing platform, accelerometers, and a GPS receiver. The computing platform continually receives input from accelerometers mounted on the car body and trucks of the rail vehicle. When the g-force output of the accelerometer exceeds set maintenance or safety-level thresholds, four seconds of acceleration data are recorded and tagged at the center location with GPS coordinates. The data collection units are programmed to report positional status information in time- and distance-based intervals to track the trains in near real-time.

The units send the recorded data directly to an Amtrak communications server via cellular digital

Amtrak's Acela Express is a high-speed train serving the Washington, D.C./New York–Boston Corridor.

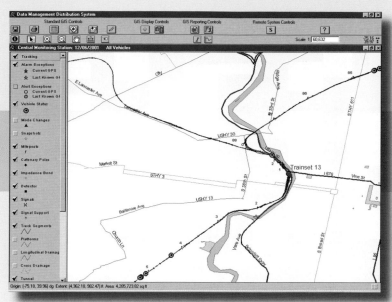

The GIS application helps Amtrak monitor ride quality information.

packet data. Generated data typically reaches the communications service in less than two minutes. Upon arrival, the data is automatically processed and input into the relational database management system where it is available for access and analysis by ArcView and the reporting system.

"With the GIS application we can pinpoint field events and relate that information to the track inspectors," said Patrick Ackroyd, track geometry engineering technician for Amtrak. "The inspectors can address the highlighted locations and fix them, if need be, on their next field inspection. The GIS works as our watchdog to provide data that will help Amtrak ensure the smoothest ride possible for our customers. At recurring ride quality problem locations, the ENSCO system helps us redirect maintenance assets to resolve the underlying causes

including bridge abutment alignment, switch alignment, and fouled subgrade."

Amtrak uses an automated custom ArcView application to analyze the ride quality information. The GIS application enables users to view the near real-time position of the vehicles, g-force values, and locations of rough riding sections of track. The application contains additional track structure and planimetric feature layers that help determine why the car is riding rough. This data includes a comprehensive survey of all track structure, mileposts, signals, over- and under-grade bridge information, interlocking locations, and switches. Users can select a safety or maintenance level event and view the waveform of the accelerations. Statistical analysis and time-based queries have been built into the GIS to help determine whether the track or vehicle is responsible for the rough ride. ⊙

Addressing application saves Texas energy company money

SECTOR *Gas and electric*
INDUSTRY *Utilities*

CenterPoint Energy
www.centerpointenergy.com

CenterPoint Energy, based in Houston, uses a custom addressing application written to facilitate its responsibility for assigning new Houston-area addresses. GIS creates the addresses and automatically transfers information about each address to the customer service information system, which creates new accounts before the customer requests service. In addition to the address, transferred information includes the results of polygon processing and coordinates used for map-based dispatching. Automation of the data feed to the customer information system saves CenterPoint Energy approximately $50,000 annually. ⊙

Automation of the data feed to the customer information system saves CenterPoint Energy approximately $50,000 annually.

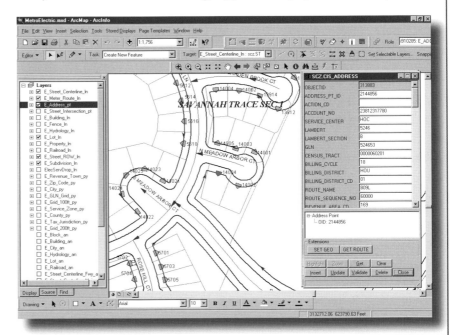

ADDITIONAL BENEFITS

Online application distributes hazardous material data fast and efficiently

Wilson, North Carolina, has adopted an online reporting system for chemical storage sites that incorporates GIS and provides a more effective and efficient means of updating and retrieving this information.

In hazardous material spills, rapid response is crucial to local fire and police departments and emergency managers. Before Wilson implemented the online reporting system, emergency workers had to access and evaluate chemical storage information and response methods manually, resulting in delayed responses.

Facilities covered by the U.S. Emergency Planning and Community Right to Know Act of 1986 must annually report the characteristics and quantities of chemicals stored on-site as well as emergency contact information. This information, known as Tier II reporting, is submitted to the State Emergency Response Commission, the Local Emergency Planning Committee, and the fire department with jurisdiction over the facility.

A majority of states, including North Carolina, rely on a manual process. When a facility submits information, it must be reviewed and filed at the state and county levels. For regions with many reporting facilities, administrators report that reviewing and filing Tier II information can take up to six months.

Accessing critical information

Recognizing the importance of maintaining and accessing this information, Wilson developed a Web-based reporting system in collaboration with Intelligent Decisions Systems, Inc. (IDSi), of Fort

SECTOR *Public safety*
INDUSTRY *Government*

Will Aycock
GIS Coordinator, City of Wilson, North Carolina
www.wilsonnc.org

Lee, New Jersey, that serves first responders, county administrators, and facility submitters.

"The application permits us to mitigate an incident more proactively, which translates into increased firefighter safety and reduction in property loss and lessens the economic impact of an event that affects the community and the environment."

—*Don Oliver*

Typically, fire departments and local emergency planning committees physically store chemical inventory records, material safety data sheets, and supplemental forms that contain vital first aid and firefighting information in binders at chemical facilities. Collecting chemical storage information scattered at various locations is difficult. Consequently, many first responders do not access Tier II chemical inventory information in emergencies. ➢

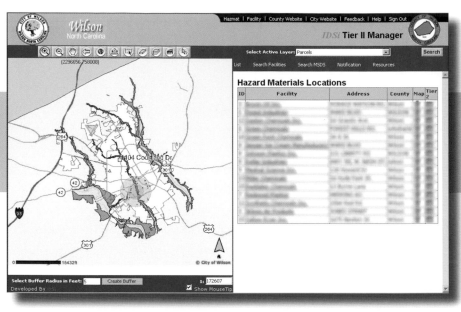

Wilson, North Carolina, has an automated online system that implements GIS to report chemical storage sites.

Wilson implemented a system that maintains chemical inventories, site plans, and chemical description information in a central database. In an emergency, first responders can access the most current facility contact, chemical inventory, material safety data sheets, site plan, and other detailed information via a secure Internet connection. The GIS component helps first respondents map the chemical facility and understand its relationship to other critical infrastructure.

The IDSi Tier II Manager was developed using Active Server Pages (ASP) and ArcIMS. Chemical storage facilities can submit and review Tier II forms more frequently than the annual filing mandated by the Right to Know Act.

"We selected ESRI's ArcIMS technology because of the easy development and customization options using ASP, ColdFusion®, Java™, JavaServer™ Pages,

and ArcXML," says Will Aycock, GIS co-coordinator for Wilson. ArcIMS provided the flexibility that enabled Wilson to develop additional Web-based applications for other departments that were implementing a citywide enterprise GIS.

Responding to an incident, emergency response planners can immediately access Tier II forms and material safety data sheets through a password-protected Web site using nothing more than a Web browser. Interactive GIS maps generated using ArcIMS are integrated into the application for planners as they formulate response strategies. The maps display a graphic presentation for the location, helping planners analyze characteristics of the affected facility and the surrounding environment.

"With our site, we are able to gain mission-critical information for incidents to which we respond in real time," said Don Oliver, Wilson's fire chief. "This is going to improve our response ability, thereby making our community safer."

The application uniquely serves the interests of private chemical companies and public emergency management authorities. Users can easily enter facility information online through a set of secure Web-enabled forms. Because this user-friendly application features easy navigation, drop-down lists, and chemical lookup tables, it encourages facility submitters to keep their data up to date. Facility submitters find the application attractive because it requires no special software. They can revise entered data as needed for review by all authorized bodies. This eliminates the need to send paper copies to multiple agencies.

"The data is gathered without requiring any additional staff time from our department," said Oliver. "The current, up-to-date information is provided by the facilities without having to be re-entered by our personnel, reducing the possibility of errors. [The IDSi Tier II Manager application] provides a more effective and more efficient means to retrieve vital information needed during crucial times in an emergency incident. The application permits us to mitigate an incident more proactively, which translates into increased firefighter safety and reduction in property loss and lessens the economic impact of an event that affects the community and the environment." ⊙

ADDITIONAL BENEFITS

BUILD AN INFORMATION BASE

Aware that knowledge is power, executives and middle managers personnel have learned that departmental and organization-wide data repositories increase institutional knowledge on projects and are excellent decision support tools. Organizing data in a GIS is advantageous because the data sets are reusable and always geographically referenced.

GIS has several advantages over traditional management information systems because it enables various disciplines to share data via geographic links. Traditional system databases use unique keys such as file number, driver's license number, customer number, social security number, or parcel identification number to link databases. GIS enables unique databases to be used by connecting geographic identifiers in a data bank such as site address, city name, ZIP Code, and service boundary. With 90 percent of all data having a geographic reference, most data can be accessed by using a geographic or location-based key.

Building a corporate information base has many benefits. An organization can draw from various disciplines and departments via a solid geographically referenced framework and increase the total number of data sets available to a project. Often different departments create and maintain the same data sets such as an address, street layer, or customer file. A GIS-based data bank provides a mechanism to eliminate or reduce this sort of data development redundancy. The information base enables businesses to produce multiple scale maps or output from a single data set. Combining data sets is an excellent way to update information, and using a centralized database can increase communication and reduce overall operational costs. More important, the ability to draw from spatially integrated data adds new dimensions to an organization's project—the ability to exchange viewpoints via GIS data or bring new data into the mix that was previously unavailable.

Being able to view and consider all pertinent data involved in a project results in informed decisions and better results. As an added benefit, cost savings will accrue because of the many users of and many uses for the centralized GIS database.

New York style mapping solutions and database tools

SECTOR *Planning*
INDUSTRY *Not for profit*

Steven Romalewski
CMAP Manager
New York Public Interest Research Group's Community
Mapping Assistance Project
www.nonprofitmaps.org

Countless New York nonprofit groups and residents have benefited from a powerful mapping and information database tool used in the work of the Community Mapping Assistance Project (CMAP), a nonprofit GIS service launched in 1997.

CMAP is a project of the New York Public Interest Research Group (NYPIRG), New York's largest nonprofit research and advocacy group. Formed twenty-seven years ago by Ralph Nader and student activists, NYPIRG works to involve citizens in government decision making on many environmental, consumer, and good government issues. The research group's goal for CMAP is to use GIS technology to help nonprofit organizations analyze issues and make a more powerful case for their causes.

Since 1997, CMAP has provided its services to more than three hundred different organizations. GIS gathers, stores, and accesses information from a single, central information base. CMAP's immense database provides topics including demographics, politics, health, historic landmarks, education, transportation, and the environment.

CMAP's GIS Web-based services have helped numerous nonprofit organizations improve services, win policy reforms, communicate better, and secure funding for valuable programs. The online services make public a wealth of information and enable organizations to embark on projects that they could not do otherwise.

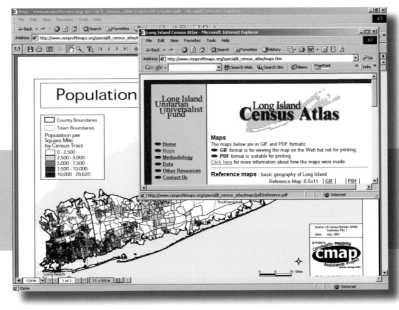

The Long Island Census Atlas includes maps, links, and information about Long Island and the 2000 Census.

Online census atlas

CMAP created the online *Census Atlas for Long Island,* which consists of static maps of 2000 Census data in GIS and PDF format for activists, policy makers, and the media. They can access these maps in a central place as a convenient starting point in their research on local demographics. The Census Atlas includes maps, links to data sources, and other information about the 2000 Census including its relevance to Long Island. Launched in December 2002, the atlas has been visited an average of five hundred times per month. The Long Island Unitarian Universalist Fund, a donor-advised fund in the Long Island Community Foundation, supported development of the atlas maps.

The maps show population patterns throughout Long Island by county and include basic reference maps showing towns and villages, population change by census tract from 1990 to 2000, population density, major race and ethnicity patterns, average household size, patterns of homeownership, and age for the population and households. The atlas also includes maps of the

Since 1997, CMAP has provided its services to more than three hundred different organizations.

Census Bureau's most recent data for Long Island, showing detailed patterns of income, poverty, education, citizenship, transportation, employment, home values, and grandparents as caregivers. This project has made it possible for hundreds of organizations to easily access and understand census data. ➤

The Community Mapping Assistance Project's *Census Atlas for Long Island* shows population patterns throughout Long Island.

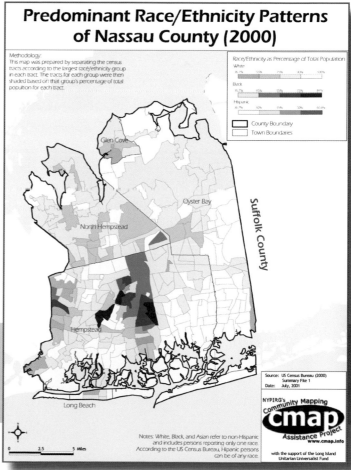

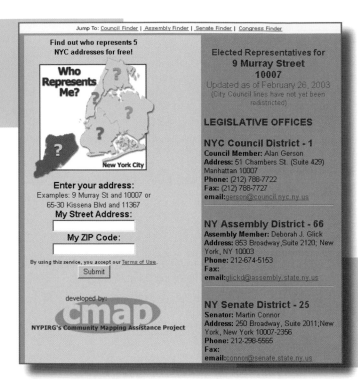

Jump To: Council Finder | Assembly Finder | Senate Finder | Congress Finder

Find out who represents 5 NYC addresses for free!

Who Represents Me?

New York City

Enter your address:
Examples: 9 Murray St and 10007 or 65-30 Kissena Blvd and 11367

My Street Address:

My ZIP Code:

By using this service, you accept our Terms of Use.

Submit

developed by:

cmap

NYPIRG's Community Mapping Assistance Project

Elected Representatives for
9 Murray Street
10007
Updated as of February 26, 2003
(City Council lines have not yet been redistricted)

LEGISLATIVE OFFICES

NYC Council District - 1
Council Member: Alan Gerson
Address: 51 Chambers St. (Suite 429) Manhattan 10007
Phone: (212) 788-7722
Fax: (212) 788-7727
email: gerson@council.nyc.ny.us

NY Assembly District - 66
Assembly Member: Deborah J. Glick
Address: 853 Broadway, Suite 2120; New York, NY 10003
Phone: 212-674-5153
Fax:
email: glickd@assembly.state.ny.us

NY Senate District - 25
Senator: Martin Connor
Address: 250 Broadway, Suite 2011; New York, New York 10007-2356
Phone: 212-298-5565
Fax:
email: connor@senate.state.ny.us

The Community Mapping Assistance Project's Web site, Who Represents Me, enables New York City residents to find and contact their public officials.

Who Represents Me

The mapping project developed Who Represents Me, a Web site to enhance NYPIRG's voter education work. "No more hunting through phone books or searching through different Web sites to find out who represents you in New York City," says Chris Meyer, NYPIRG's executive director. "Now NYPIRG provides one-stop shopping access to government at the local, state, and federal levels. This Internet site enables the public to easily find and contact their representatives about the environmental, consumer, good government, and transit issues NYPIRG works on." The latest version of Who Represents Me includes an expansion to cover elected officials on Long Island. The New York Community Trust and the Long Island Unitarian Universalist Fund support the project.

The Who Represents Me service is unique in that no other organization provides New York residents with such an accessible, comprehensive, one-stop service. It is also an example of how GIS Web-based technology can improve access to government.

Mapping lead poisoning

CMAP also showed the occurrence of lead poisoning in New York City's children. Working with CMAP, NYPIRG health advocates from the research group used this data to prepare a report calling on the city council to renew its focus on lead poisoning prevention.

The report made a powerful and immediate impact upon its release in June 2002. The *New York Times* and other newspapers reproduced the maps. Within weeks of the report's release, the city council's minority caucus held a special hearing on the issue. The caucus prominently displayed the research group's maps and referred to them repeatedly during the hearing, providing a clear picture of the importance of the issue in member districts. The minority caucus adopted a resolution to make passage of strong legislation a top priority. The full council passed the lead poisoning bill, and sent it to Mayor Michael Bloomberg for his approval. Advocates and public officials use the Mapping Lead Poisoning project to make decisions on important policy and budget issues.

Many projects benefit all New Yorkers

The Council on the Environment of New York City asked CMAP to develop an online Community Garden Locator *(www.cenyc.org)* to provide information about neighborhood community gardens. Gardeners can locate their gardens on the interactive maps and update information about hours of operation, plants grown at the garden, and events. It might have taken the council months to collect this information were it not for the Community Garden Locator. Hundreds of gardeners across the city use the site.

The Metropolitan Waterfront Alliance used CMAP maps of current and proposed ferry routes in New York harbor to help convince the New York City Council to allocate $300,000 in the 2001 budget to study the deployment of a comprehensive ferry system linking Brooklyn to Manhattan and New Jersey.

CMAP has provided mapping services to several philanthropic foundations including the Robin Hood Foundation, the J.M. Kaplan Fund, and the New York Women's Foundation. Trustees of these groups can determine if grants are made in areas of greatest financial need and if they reach the target audience.

The Brooklyn Public Library has begun using CMAP's analysis of census data to determine if branch libraries are serving intended populations most effectively and to compare usage statistics—youth readership and non-English language materials—with local population patterns. ⊙

"*NYPIRG CMAP gives nonprofit groups and local communities a window on their world that would've been daunting, at best, for the average citizen or neighborhood group to obtain without access to GIS. We're able to leverage support from ESRI and other software companies, private foundations, and myriad public and private data sources to create mapping tools that otherwise would have been out of reach for our nonprofit, philanthropic, and public-sector partners.*"

Steven Romalewski

ADDITIONAL BENEFITS

Improved land-use mapping

SECTOR *Planning*
INDUSTRY *Government*

Steve Waldron
GIS Coordinator, City of Richmond, Virginia
www.ci.richmond.va.us

In Richmond, Virginia, the Division of Land Use Administration is responsible for amending the zoning ordinance and supporting the Board of Zoning Appeals and the Planning Commission. One staff member, the drafting technician, creates zoning maps, land-use maps, and master plan maps for the city's Board of Zoning Appeals and the Planning Commission.

Until 2001, the drafting technicians had been using the same process for the past twenty years—filing cabinets, outdated paper map documents, and legacy mainframes. Using the paper method meant they had to do everything manually or outsource to a vendor. It proved difficult and time-consuming to meld information that arrived from multiple sources and in differing scales and formats. To improve this process Richmond implemented a GIS to build a geographic database.

Richmond's GIS started with ArcView 3 to prepare the property, zoning, land use, and master plan maps. GIS compiles necessary information into one place, saving staff members time and effort. They subsequently ported these functions to ArcGIS, and GIS staff developed a custom ArcGIS application that enables users to query a specific address; zoom to a desired geographical extent; and create a site, zoning, existing land use, or master plan land-use map with a date and scale bar.

A new data view created in ArcGIS contained the zoning district data file. Using the query builder, all the residential districts (e.g., single family, multi-family, mobile home, and residential–office) were selected and converted to a new residential district data file. A similar process selected other zoned areas and created separate data files.

The project uses layers for parcel, zoning, master plan land use, transportation, surface parking lots, and the existing land use. The parcel layer is powerful because its features are directly linked to the Assessor's Office and central address

Incorporated in 1782, Richmond has many cultural and historical landmarks.

databases. Users can directly access address, ownership, property values, and land-use information by clicking on a parcel without any time-consuming research. The drafting technician can query a complete, citywide representation of property boundaries and, by zooming in or out, view spatially correct property lines. After labeling streets and properties, the drafting technician simply turns on the zoning, existing land use, or master plan land-use layers and can print any of these maps.

GIS technology gave the Division of Land Use Administration an opportunity to replace archaic

The city regards GIS technology as a productivity tool.

methods and build a modern geographic information database that brings together land-use information. The success of the GIS projects has encouraged continued implementation inside the division. The city regards GIS technology as a productivity tool. With GIS, the staff has optimized existing work processes to perform new business processes, accomplish assigned tasks, and support the decision-making process. ⊙

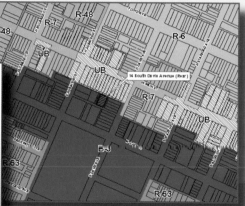

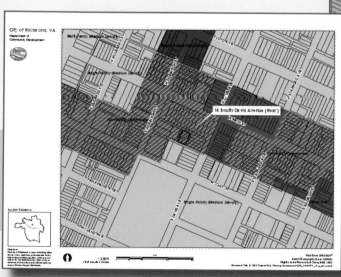

Richmond's GIS saves staff members time and effort in preparing property, zoning, land use, and master plan maps.

ADDITIONAL BENEFITS

Virtual land management

SECTOR Gas and electric
INDUSTRY Utilities

CenterPoint Energy
www.centerpointenergy.com

CenterPoint Energy's Land and Right-of-Way Division serves as property manager for 70,885 acres of land within the Houston metropolitan area. CenterpPoint Energy seeks to maximize the revenue and nonrevenue benefits from real property assets, prevent adverse effects from primary use, minimize risk and liabilities, and minimize the cost to manage and own property. While regular field visits to all of the company's holdings are costly and logistically impossible, CenterPoint Energy's GIS efficiently manages the property by bringing all available data about the property to desktop computers. Data, such as how the asset was purchased, current uses of the asset, its physical boundaries, and the acreage within the asset, is readily available to agents. GIS assists the Land and Right-of-Way Division in managing approximately $9 million of annual revenue. The GIS information base saves about $80,000 per year in land and right-of-way labor costs. ⊙

> *The GIS information base saves about $80,000 per year in land and right-of-way labor costs.*

CenterPoint Energy maintains its property assets and manages its property rights-of-way with GIS.

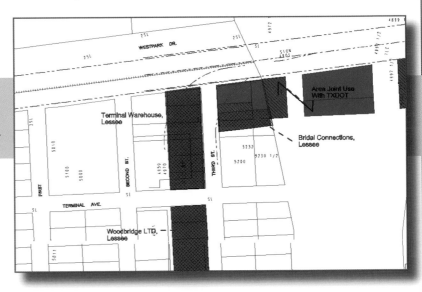

ADDITIONAL BENEFITS

MANAGE RESOURCES

Efficient resource management means analyzing, tracking, managing, allocating, and conserving assets. Enhanced resource management might involve influencing the way a corporation uses its assets, or it can take on a broader context to include managing the earth's precious commodities to sustain our world. Applications of resource planning occur in all disciplines.

For quick and efficient production and delivery, many companies and agencies have cultivated enterprise resource planning technology. This technology helps to streamline, analyze, and automate business processes such as accounting, inventory, e-commerce, human resources, sales, shipping, and customer service. These companies are integrating GIS with their resource planning technology systems to maximize benefits and effectively manage resources.

In an emergency, utilities must quickly mobilize staff, equipment, and supplies. Integrating various systems and work processes streamlines the effort. The customer relationship management system helps to collect customer calls related to an outage, the outage management system identifies the point(s) of failure, enterprise resource planning ensures the dispatch of necessary resources, and the GIS integrates information to optimize travel routes.

GIS, integrated with enterprise resource planning and business processes, benefits businesses and governments as a decision support tool that sustains our earth and impacts costs, productivity gains, inventory control, and staffing.

The success of resource management depends on understanding how geography and its related elements affect commodities. Start by asking where assets are located. Then look for the origin of the demand for these assets, or which local issues or climates affect the resource.

Agribusiness uses GIS to study crop yield by location to understand the logistics of getting products to market. Businesses use GIS to assign workers based on geographic demand for a service. Local agencies meet homeland security guidelines by scheduling an event near resources that might be needed in a disaster.

Managing land records in New Mexico

SECTOR *Cadastral*
INDUSTRY *Government*

GIS Technology, Inc.
www.gistech.com

In 2003, Patrick H. Lyons, the newly elected commissioner of Public Lands at the New Mexico State Land Office (SLO) confronted the challenge of managing nine million acres of surface and thirteen million acres of subsurface land scattered across thirty-two of New Mexico's thirty-three counties.

By 1910, Congress had granted to New Mexico trust lands consisting of nearly 12 percent of the state's land. SLO administers these lands for the benefit of public institutions, primarily public schools. In marketing and managing trust lands, SLO deals with millions of lease and title records

and growing demands to serve the public, trust beneficiaries, and lessees of public lands fairly and efficiently.

As an elected official, Lyons had a statutory obligation to preserve the trust, which has increasingly become an issue of sustainable management. It is no longer acceptable for information to stay filed away in cabinets and employees' desks. Decision makers need quick access to information in a demanding market. GIS, tightly integrated with document and tabular data management systems, provides information for timely and effective land management. Customer service is paramount for Commissioner Lyons and SLO.

Prior to GIS implementation, the New Mexico State Land Office used a tedious record keeping system.

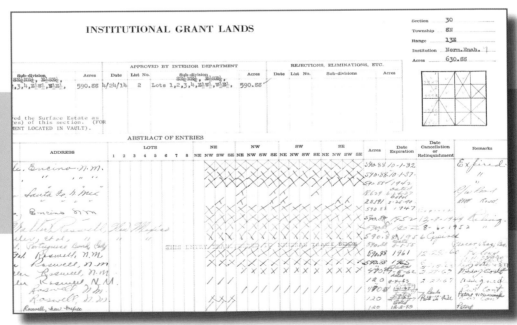

Tediously keeping track

Since its inception, the State Land Office used a system to organize lease and title records based on the Public Land Survey grid. Paper ledgers, called tract books, record all lease transactions and title documents by town, range, and section. When a lease is created, assigned, expired, or acted on in any way, entries are made in every tract book containing some record of the leased property. The tract book entries refer to paper documents stored in folders.

In the early 1990s, the State Land Office began supplementing the paper-based records system with a database application written in DB2® called ONGARD. The database preserves the section-indexing scheme that originated with the paper system. While logical and appropriate when it was designed, the paper-based system imposes many burdens. Duplicate records must be posted in the tract

A simple query that might have previously taken hours now takes seconds.

books, often on many different pages, and entered in ONGARD. The growing number of paper records posed a storage and security challenge. Maintaining the physical integrity of the records and restricting access to authorized personnel are concerns because some of the records are not public information.

More important, staff often found it difficult to access needed information to do their jobs. An employee who receives a request to modify a lease might have to research the tract books and ONGARD for information. This could require looking through many pages of many tract books before checking out the necessary documents. Staff members often checked out documents for several months while completing the request. ➤

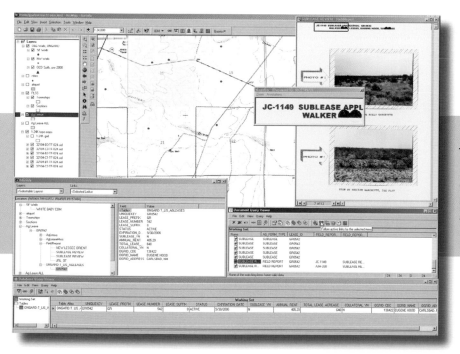

The new system, which integrates GIS technology, digitally stores documents and provides for easy access to them.

The system also limited developers because it lacked a method to quickly search for trust properties with specific spatial characteristics, such as proximity to paved roads or a particular soil type. Information on public records required a trip to Santa Fe or a special request for records. It also cost money to retrieve and copy records and time to process and mail requests. The records provided some information about a specific property but offered no spatial context. Determining proximity to features such as roads was difficult.

New system checks out

Seeking efficient information storage and management coupled with improved access to data, Lyons and the SLO staff turned to ESRI and its business partner GIS Technology, Inc. (GTI). ESRI and its partner delivered key technology components, including ArcGIS and FileNET's Panagon document management system.

The document management system solved the document storage and retrieval problems. The system secured scanned paper records and electronic documents, such as reports and correspondence, in the Panagon document repository with appropriate access limitations. Authorized staff members can retrieve documents from anywhere on the network or the Internet. They can annotate or redact documents, subject to authorization constraints.

The document annotation capability provides a way to preserve "institutional memory" about state lands. When documents are added to the system, document metadata is also added that enables query-based document retrieval.

Instead of tediously searching ONGARD and the tract books, users can access lease and title information through ArcGIS. GIS provides the critical spatial context for state-owned lands, enhancing decision making.

The GTI system combines GIS with the document repository and tabular information drawn from the ONGARD system and enables users to query all three information sources in an integrated fashion. A state lands employee searching for available grazing land near currently leased property can retrieve lease documents from the document management system and create a map display that shows the lease boundary and surrounding area with a single menu pick. Using GIS to select other nearby properties, the employee can link back to the system and ONGARD tables to determine the availability of the selected lands.

A query can start in GIS, ONGARD, or the document management system. State lands employees can use the selection to retrieve information from the other systems. A simple query that might have previously taken hours now takes seconds. Because of integrated access, state land employees can find information without knowing if it is in a table or a document. Moreover, complex queries involving spatial relationships, which were practically impossible before, are now available. ◉

ADDITIONAL BENEFITS

Open space project provides public outreach

SECTOR *Planning*
INDUSTRY *Not for profit*

Matt Arnn
Project Director, USDA Forest Service
www.oasisnyc.net

The Open Accessible Space Information System (OASIS) provides widespread access to maps and information about New York City's parks, community gardens, wetlands, beaches, greenways, and waterways. OASIS is a coalition led by the U.S. Department of Agriculture (USDA) Forest Service consisting of more than forty nonprofit organizations, businesses, government agencies, and academic institutions.

OASIS, New York City's only interactive GIS data sharing Web site for green infrastructure, is a mapping application that helps communities develop a better understanding of their environmental resources with interactive maps of open spaces, census data, property information, and transportation networks.

The New York Public Interest Research Group is New York State's largest consumer, environmental, and government reform organization. In late 2000, the USDA Forest Service and OASIS steering committee selected the research group's Community Mapping Assistance Project to develop the OASIS Web site using ESRI's ArcIMS technology. Launched in May 2001, the site provides access to approximately forty-eight layers of spatial data about the city's green infrastructure.

Specific OASIS projects include assisting in the USDA Forest Service Living Memorials Initiative, a tree inventory, and a habitat information study. Users accessed the site more than one million times in one year. OASIS has won several local public service awards. ⊙

The New York Public Interest Research Group developed the Open Accessible Space Information System to provide information about New York City's parks and open space.

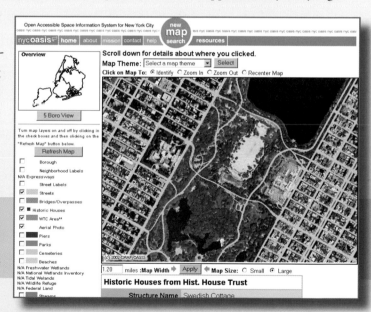

ADDITIONAL BENEFITS

Coordinating street projects saves California county money

SECTOR *Public works*
INDUSTRY *Government*

Mark Perry
GeoPrise.Net
www.geoprise.net

Sacramento County's Public Works Department GIS developed an intranet-based application using ArcIMS that improved communication within the department. By coordinating street work, the county consolidated projects—saving both time and money. Readily accessible information and proactive notification, two features of the Project Coordination application, helped managers make better decisions. The county also created Parcel Viewer, Mailing List Generator, and Sewer Infrastructure Viewer applications. These applications and several other applications in development will eventually be available to the public via the Internet.

> *Preventing one unnecessary cul-de-sac overlay in Sacramento County more than justifies the cost.*

How does a government agency provide real-time project information and service to employees and the public? Have you ever driven through a neighborhood and noticed the same street dug up several times in a short period? Or have you ever found a freshly overlaid street being trenched?

Organizational silos remain pervasive, despite the re-engineering trends of the 1990s. Cross-organizational communication typically remains secondary to immediate project responsibilities. In addition, the fiber optics boom created a backlog of construction projects and a stockpile of planning and development studies. Staffing shortages in engineering and planning organizations add to the problem.

Sacramento County found a solution in the Street Excavation in Right-of-Way (SEROW) application of ArcIMS. This Web-based coordination tool enables users to produce maps of current and planned projects that involve street excavation in the right-of-way and perform spatial and tabular queries for reports. Engineers, planners, developers, utilities, governing boards, and the public use this application.

The application includes powerful online tools to create and maintain project data and an automated e-mail notification process that tracks project data status. If someone creates conflicting data, the application triggers an automated e-mail to contacts listed for the affected projects.

Sacramento County put SEROW on its intranet for anyone with a browser and a network connection. Users access project data through spatial and tabular searches. To access data via a spatial search, users zoom and pan to the geographic area of interest, trigger the rendering of projects, and click a project to open a new window that presents a tabular display of project data. To access data via a tabular search, users open the project search screen and define search criteria.

An organization must commit staff to maintain project data using the online administration tools, but the return on investment quickly justifies the minimum required efforts. It would cost about $10,000 for an associate-level engineer to update every project record in the SEROW database in one year. That compares to about $20,000 to overlay a short residential cul-de-sac in Sacramento County. Preventing one unnecessary cul-de-sac overlay in Sacramento County more than justifies the cost. Imagine the tremendous savings when the application prevents duplicate work on a large-scale project.

Besides monetary savings, other significant benefits of this application include improved communication and coordination among government agencies, developers, and utilities; reduction in public inconvenience; and enhanced customer service. ⊙

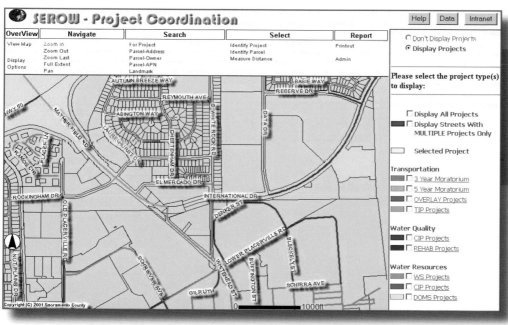

Coordinating street work with GIS within Sacramento County helps to consolidate projects and save time and money.

ADDITIONAL BENEFITS

Stormy weather doesn't slow city

SECTOR *Public safety*
INDUSTRY *Government*

City of Schaumburg, Illinois
www.ci.schaumburg.il.us

In 2001, GIS Solutions, Inc. (G/I/S), designed, developed, and implemented a custom GIS application to automate snow command center operations for the Public Works Department in Schaumburg, Illinois.

The application enables snow command personnel to manage and track snow-fighting efforts and resources during a snowstorm or ice storm. The software tracks completion status and assigned locations for vehicles and personnel. Operators can change driver and vehicle snowplow assignments, monitor completion times and the status of snowplow routes, and log resident concerns and complaints received on a snow-fighting hotline. Supervisors and managers use the process to track employee and equipment hours, produce summary reports for snow-fighting costs, and review snow-fighting efforts when a storm has passed. The GIS application saves images of maps created during snow operations for public use as well as internal review of snow command efforts.

The application was developed using ArcObjects software from ESRI and Visual Basic. Operators, supervisors, and managers use the application

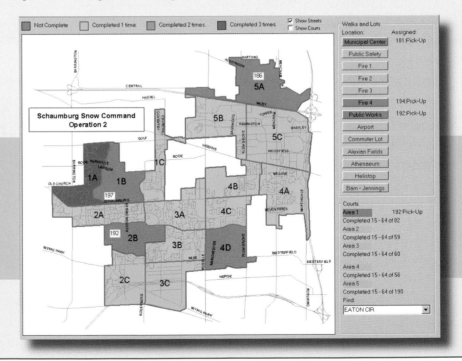

installed on three separate machines. Each machine accesses a geodatabase that stores geographic information including basemaps, route locations, completion status, and vehicle locations. A Microsoft Access database stores operational and historic data created during a storm. Interfaces built in Visual Basic capture data about snow-fighting efforts and vehicle data maintenance. Historic storm data including cost totals, employee and vehicle assignment, and completion can also be viewed using interfaces to this database.

Schaumburg began using the application during the first snowstorm on December 17, 2001. Of the twenty-six storms that season, three required three days or more of continuous snow-fighting efforts. The software tracked different types of resources, such as employee overtime hours, and maintained a list of employees to call and the number of vehicles in operation during a storm or on a particular day. Automated reports, generated almost immediately after a storm passed, calculated total costs of storm snow fighting by storm, day, work shift, week, and month.

Internet users can view a status map that is updated every fifteen minutes during a storm and receive detailed locations of snow-removal efforts at the Schaumburg Web site *(www.ci.schaumburg.il.us/ snowcommand)*. ◉

The software can track different types of resources, such as employee overtime hours, maintain a list of employees to call, and calculate the number of vehicles in operation during a storm or on a particular day.

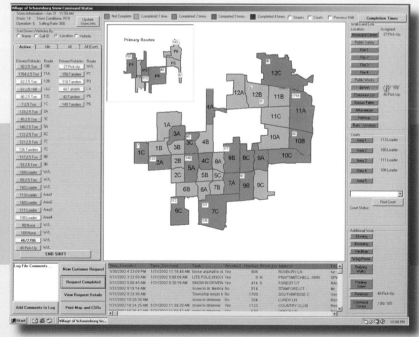

IMPROVE ACCESS TO GOVERNMENT

Government agencies have found an ideal way to extend their services—GIS on the Internet. Nearly 90 percent of all inquiries that governments receive are geographically related. This leaves little doubt that linking a mapping interface to a government Web site will move e-government (government services online) closer to a more interactive and informative process.

Not knowing where to initiate a request and the angst of dealing with bureaucracy led to years of distrust on the part of citizenry. Government needed to improve its image, and many agencies began to seek ways to improve access to service.

Playing an increasingly vital role, GIS in e-government is strengthening governments' ability to generate greater efficiencies in operations, serve citizens, improve education, broaden outreach, and compete globally. Most important, e-government supports a range of relationships that include government-to-government, citizens-to-government, business-to-government, and internal communications.

The benefits are mounting as more governments implement GIS as a portal to the public. Early indications of the payback were realized when data portals aided in improving communication and reducing the need for data redundancy. Available twenty-four hours a day, seven days a week, e-government has saved time by reducing necessary trips to government offices. Citizen approval has increased, and with increased access, more people are involved in the government process.

Geospatial One-Stop portal is keystone to e-government strategy

SECTOR *Administration/Management*
INDUSTRY *Government*

U.S. Office of Management and Budget
www.geo-one-stop.gov

The Bush Administration made a commitment to technology, which is detailed in the E-Government Act signed by President George W. Bush in 2002. It calls for expanded use of the Internet and computer resources to deliver government services in a citizen-centered, results-oriented, and market-based government. For assistance in this effort, the Office of Management and Budget oversees twenty-four e-government initiatives that will enhance government efficiency. The Geospatial One-Stop Initiative is one of them.

The cost savings realized through this "build once, use many times" application is exactly the vision of the Office of Management and Budget's e-government initiatives.

The purpose of Geospatial One-Stop is twofold—to support the business of government and decision making. Government generally supports disaster management, recreation, planning, homeland security, public health, and environmental protection. Each has a geographic component and requires geospatial data to be managed appropriately. In decision making, officials make choices about certain events, such as floods, fires, or crimes, which might have broader implications, sometimes affecting entire communities. Geospatial information gives decision makers the ability to see data in a community context and facilitate cross-agency coordination.

Geospatial One-Stop builds on investments already made in the National Spatial Data Infrastructure and capitalizes on advances in geospatial information technologies. The initiative encourages greater collaboration and coordination of spatial data at all levels of government. Of its several components, the most visible is a portal for easier, faster, and less-expensive government and public access to geospatial information.

Portal development

Many components of government, such as disaster relief and security, require quick and easy access to accurate, up-to-date data. The Geospatial One-Stop team designed the portal as an Internet-based organizational umbrella for federal agencies producing and accessing geospatial data. The portal or gateway is a repository for spatial data and Web services that support local, state, and federal programs. It is a network of distributed networks providing searchable local, state, and federal data; planned data development activities; map services; problem solving applications; data collection activities; references; contact information about GIS professionals; standards; and geospatial best practices.

The Geospatial One-Stop team delivered a fully functional portal in a matter of weeks by working with developers at ESRI who had already done successful work in this area for the National Integrated Land System project at the Bureau of Land Management and the Geography Network. The project's GeoCommunicator portal provided a perfect time-saving and money-saving jumpstart to develop the Geospatial One-Stop portal. The ESRI team assisted in quickly creating the portal, which is based on standard, commercial off-the-shelf technology and incorporates industry-approved open, interoperable standards. Geospatial One-Stop launched in June 2003.

Its users are now able to

- search the network for Web services, images, geographic data sets, contacts, activities, and clearinghouses;
- register for notification when new or updated data, maps, activities, and references have been added in specific search areas;
- view metadata to determine if the data is suitable for the intended use;
- access available geographic data and Web services directly through the portal;
- download large data sets from providers through feature streaming or FTP services;
- publish (register) map services, images, geographic data sets, geoservices, spatial solutions, geographic and land reference material, and geographic activities or events to share with others via online provider forms. ➢

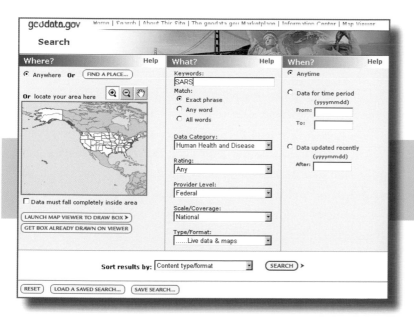

Geospatial One-Stop users can search the network and view maps customized to their specifications.

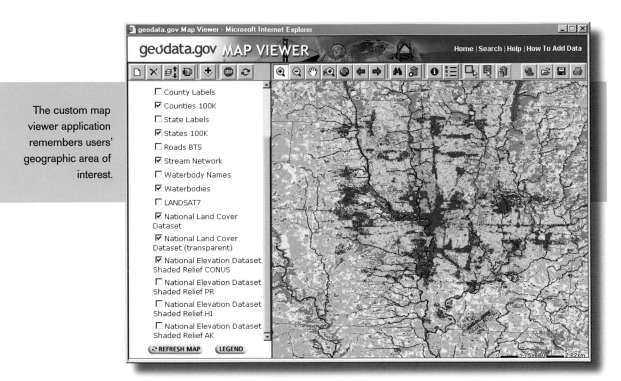

The custom map viewer application remembers users' geographic area of interest.

Innovations are key

Flexibility and innovation are key to keeping pace with the business of government. Many Geospatial One-Stop features exemplify these characteristics.

Channel

Users who want an easy way to find data about the environment and agriculture can click on the agriculture channel and switch to the environment channel. Channels enable users to organize data, applications, best practices, projects, and users by theme or topic. This strategy provides shortcuts and creates an online meeting place for those interested in specific topics such as agriculture, emergency management, or land records. As the Geospatial One-Stop portal matures, more channels will be added. Topic experts can "own" the channel and keep its content current. This kind of structure encourages the inclusion of the best available data regardless of the originator. Channels are a practical vehicle for engaging a broad user community that can collectively populate the portal with data.

Map viewer

The portal's custom map viewer gives users the ability to easily overlay new data layers by changing channels. As the user searches for and adds new data to the view, the application remembers the geographic area of interest. There is no need to zoom again.

Basemap selection

Basemaps put features in context. To save time, the Geospatial One-Stop portal offers *The National Map* from the U.S. Geological Survey as a standard basemap of the entire United States. This enables portal users to quickly orient themselves and provides a base upon which they can overlay information of their choice. The National Map includes thematic layers such as roads, hydrography, land cover, elevation, administrative boundaries, and place names.

Metadata harvesting

A new metadata warehouse and search tool are on hand at the portal. The repository is based on the concept of harvesting metadata from distributed clearinghouse nodes to a structured storage area enabling fast, reliable results. Only the metadata is harvested, and the actual data and Web services remain at the original host site.

Applying e-government initiatives

The Geospatial One-Stop portal's design is based on a mandate for efficiency and cost savings, and as such, it supports other federal e-government initiatives. Recreation One-Stop uses the mapping functionality of the portal to meet its business needs. *Disasterhelp.gov* can also use the standard basemaps served up through the portal as a foundation to map emergency incidents. The cost savings realized through this "build once, use many times" application is exactly the vision of the Office of Management and Budget's e-government initiatives.

The Geospatial One-Stop program is the foundation for building a GIS for the nation as it responds to a variety of federal directives demanding better service to citizens, more collaboration, and improved efficiency and homeland security. All citizens are encouraged to participate in Geospatial One-Stop. To start, go to *www.geodata.gov.* ◉

ADDITIONAL BENEFITS

Constituents benefit from Los Angeles County Web-based property assessment system

SECTOR *Cadastral*
INDUSTRY *Government*

Emilio Solano
Chief Cadastral Engineer
Office of Los Angeles County Assessor, California

Administering any county government is a complex and intricate endeavor. The complexities amplify in larger counties, and burgeoning populations make the challenges even greater.

Los Angeles County's 4,084 square miles cover an area larger than the combined states of Delaware and Rhode Island. It is the most populous county in the nation, with an estimated ten million people. Charged with providing an array of services, county officials regularly juggle the likes of property assessment, law enforcement, social services, and specialized support systems. As departments strive to operate at maximum efficiency, the county Assessor's Office is getting a strong boost in that direction from Internet GIS. Savings in time, money, and resources are soaring while county constituents benefit with increased information access.

Assessing tax rolls—no small task

The Assessor's Office is a branch of the county's Property Taxation System. Other branches include the Registrar–Recorder, Auditor–Controller, and Treasurer–Tax Collector. The assessor's responsibilities include locating and identifying property ownership, establishing property values, completing an assessment roll, applying all legal exemptions, and providing public information. The Assessor's Mapping Services section serves under the Assessor's Office.

For decades, the Assessors Office recorded ownership and property tax data sets on thousands of paper maps that span the county. Property and tax maps were only available to citizens who visited the Assessor's Office and made requests for hard-copy information.

The Assessor's Mapping Services section began automating its mapmaking and editing efforts with GIS in the late 1980s. The organization grew and matured along with its ideas for GIS technology. In 1997, Mapping Services acquired ArcIMS to provide the public with easy access to data via the Internet.

"We wanted to provide a service to constituents that made parcel and property value information available so they could make informed decisions," said Richard N. Quacquarini, chief cadastral engineer, Office of Los Angeles County Assessor's Mapping Services section. "We wanted something that was intuitive and user-friendly and provided the targeted functionality whether a user has a slower dial-up connection or a faster broadband connection."

ArcGIS, ArcSDE, and ArcView 3.2 are integral parts of two system configurations. One system is on-site providing production needs, and the other is off-site providing Web applications. The assessor's system is called the Property Assessment Information System (PAIS). Users access PAIS through a standard Web browser to research assessment information for individual parcels, print the assessor's maps, and search for sales within the last two years. They can pan, zoom, and view indexed parcel information including property values, parcel numbers, and sales data.

Whether running a query based on a parcel number, address, or street intersection or merely panning and zooming around a map, viewers can quickly access linked assessor information via digital maps on the Web. The assessor contacted ESRI to help in the development of PAIS, which includes data from Rand McNally, Thomas Bros. Maps, and the county Department of Public Works. The site also features a link to the Treasurer–Tax Collector's Web page.

The Web site enables a real estate agent to select a subject property and buffer out five hundred and one thousand feet or one-fourth, one-half, and one mile to identify properties that have sold in the last two years. Real estate professionals account for a significant amount of the assessor's public service counter traffic because they regularly need to establish acceptable buying and selling prices on

Savings in time, money, and resources are soaring while county constituents benefit with increased information access.

properties. A real estate agent can identify comparable properties (with similar square footage, bedrooms, and baths) to determine a baseline selling price. These professionals would normally have to telephone the Assessor's Office or visit the Registrar–Recorder's Office to get this information.

PAIS features a seamless GIS parcel map base with links to scanned versions of the actual hardcopy assessment maps. It enables users to quickly link to scanned maps for legal description information and lot dimensions. It is an example of true public access, with ArcIMS providing the technology architecture to access detailed map data. The successful site represents a huge savings in public counter labor costs. In October 2001, soon after the site was unveiled, the site logged four million page views with 1.4 million map requests. This represented eighty thousand actual visits to the site by twenty thousand unique visitors. ⊙

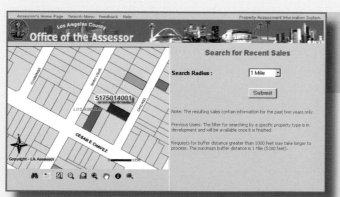

The Los Angeles County Assessor provides online information including maps for the public for access, query, and analysis.

ADDITIONAL BENEFITS

Showcasing Tucson's economic potential

SECTOR *Economic development*
INDUSTRY *Government*

GIS Planning, Inc.
Office of Economic Development, City of Tucson, Arizona
www.gisplanning.com

To develop sensible yet economically viable planning strategies, urban planners and business investors rely on information about urban characteristics such as demographics, utility infrastructure, and economic incentive zones. GIS makes this information immediately accessible, and the software offers decision makers key geographic perspectives for demonstrating and modeling the economic possibilities of a region.

The Office of Economic Development (OED) for Tucson, Arizona, uses GIS to help businesses locate available commercial space in town. Its Web-based GIS application brings together information that identifies Tucson's commercial property potential. OED contracted with ESRI business partner GIS Planning, Inc., to assist with the design and development of the application, which uses ArcIMS software and GIS data created by the city's GIS cooperative.

Called Commercial Property Online, this Web site enables visitors to search for commercial properties based on a variety of criteria including size, type of building, location, special economic incentive zones, and demographics. The secure Web interface gives registered real estate brokers the ability to add, modify, or delete property information. The site provides maps of selected properties, lot characteristics or building facilities, and utility infrastructure information and generates standard and custom demographic and business reports. In addition, the site displays an aerial photo of each site when a user selects a property. After identifying a property, the site displays other information, including searchable demographic and business license information, assessor tax data, and utility infrastructure information.

Economic development professionals for community planning also use Commercial Property Online. The site promotes infill and discourages urban sprawl by showing areas with existing infrastructure and encouraging growth in these areas. By choosing sites with available infrastructure, companies can avoid the costly expense of bringing basic services to sites. This tool gives city planners, chambers of commerce, and economic development agencies the ability to see the overall picture of service delivery and the entire pattern of commercial development within the community.

Businesses and investors have positively received this professional looking, interactive Web site that reflects well on a city striving to promote a progressive image. ⊙

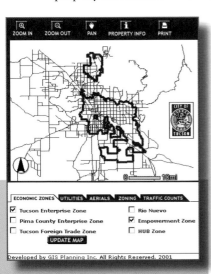

Visitors to Tucson's Commercial Property Online can search for business properties based on a variety of criteria.

Web mapping helps county provide social services

Westchester County, New York, covers approximately 450 square miles and is situated just north of New York City. It became one of the first counties in the state to establish a GIS project to develop, maintain, and distribute digital data. In 1988, the county implemented a program to provide GIS outreach to local governments, which provides technical assistance and guidance.

SECTOR *Planning*
INDUSTRY *Government*

Deborah Parker
Westchester County, New York
www.westchestergov.com

With rolling hills and streams, Westchester County is one of the most heavily forested in New York. While northern Westchester County has retained much of its rural charm, communities in the southern part of the county, influenced by their highly urbanized neighbor, New York City, are growing more quickly. The 2000 Census showed that Westchester County's population was at its highest ever—nearly one million. Subsequently, demand for county social services is on the rise.

Internet application identifies community services

With GIS applications in place for planning, assessment, and public works, Westchester County GIS has expanded its capabilities to include Web-mapping programs for social and human services.

Service delivery locations are identified and built as GIS coverages based on address files from agencies responsible for administering the service delivery programs. The coverages are merged into the county's ArcIMS Web-based mapping environment, and the application, Community Facility and Services Locator (CFSL), is accessible via the county's GIS Web site.

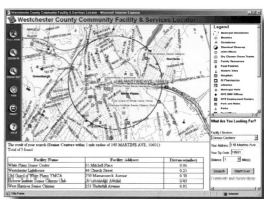

This Westchester County Internet GIS enables users to search for various community services that are located within a specific radius of an address.

CFSL includes information for programs covering youth services, children's mental health services, and the Westchester Coalition for the Hungry and Homeless, Inc. (WCHH). Coalition data contains the locations and contact information for area soup kitchens, shelters, and food pantries.

Rosa Boone, executive director of WCHH said, "By providing up-to-date, current locations of the seventy-two food pantries, thirty-eight soup kitchens, and thirty-three shelters under its umbrella, WCHH gives needy families in the twenty-four communities easier access to such services." County GIS staffers are reviewing requests from local governments to expand the online mapping and listing neighborhood programs that serve residents in specific communities. ⊙

ADDITIONAL BENEFITS

Mapping the vote

SECTOR *Elections*
INDUSTRY *Government*

Kevin Blake
Coordinator, Yavapai County, Arizona
mapserver.co.yavapai.az.us/gis/yavgis

Among the most common excuses for not voting is, "I don't know which precinct I'm in," or "I don't know where to go to vote." Yavapai County, Arizona, residents have no reason to use those excuses.

In this rural Arizona county, GIS is helping the democratic process. Yavapai County is located northwest of Phoenix. Encompassing more than eight thousand square miles, it is approximately the size of New Jersey. Its landscape varies from vast stretches of desert to scrubland and forest. Home to some of the most striking desert landscapes imaginable, Yavapai County affords its 155,000 residents plenty of elbow room.

The GIS department helps county citizens locate the jurisdictions where they live and vote. The scattered population complicates a seemingly simple task. Odd-shaped districts rarely line up neatly, and neighbors living side by side sometimes reside in different electoral districts. Nevertheless, representational government mandates the election of a governing body from districts that are relatively equal in population.

With the Yavapai County Election Map tool, by picking and choosing among layers, residents can build maps to find their supervisorial, judicial, legislative, or college districts.

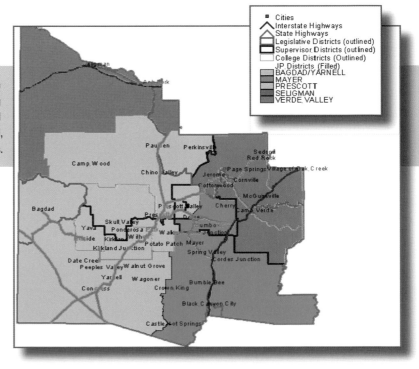

The county's GIS-based Election Map Tool enables users to view layers of information and see the relationships between each of the features.

The Election Map Tool integrates several different Arizona electoral districts as layers. By picking and choosing among layers, residents can build their own maps to find their geographic place within supervisory, judicial, legislative, or college districts. For the Election Map Tool, the GIS department wanted users to be able to choose from different layers, a simple task with the frame enabling capabilities of the ArcIMS templates.

Yavapai's Internet map services filled a need in this unique land and community. The county Web

The county Web site receives twelve thousand hits a month, and ten thousand of those are for GIS map services proving that citizens in Yavapai are interested and accessing information available to them.

site receives twelve thousand hits a month, and ten thousand of those are for GIS map services proving that citizens in Yavapai are interested and accessing information available to them. GIS has enabled this without undue stress on taxpayer-funded resources. ⊙

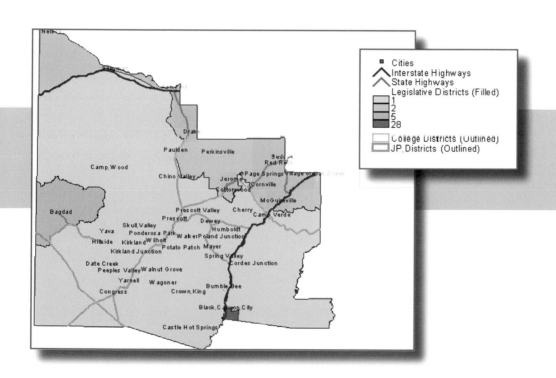

ENTERPRISE GIS

The business case for GIS is based on an organization's understanding of how to apply the technology to meet its business goals and objectives. Organizations realize benefits from GIS as they apply the technology to re-engineer processes and solve problems.

Organizations often look for examples of GIS applications to help them understand what the software can do. While this is helpful in developing a program based on tried and true methods, the benefits of GIS come from an institution's constant quest to push the limits of spatial analyses.

Different applications of GIS yield varying rates of return, and it is common to seek the "killer application" for the largest return on investment or to justify the expenditure. Examples of GIS business processes yielding phenomenal benefits abound. An organization can achieve a more significant and sustaining return on investment once every division of the group understands and applies the technology. Moving a GIS program from a department-wide to an organization-wide operation will yield the maximum return.

Some benefits of an applied GIS are more quantifiable than others, and single GIS projects often produce many benefits valued differently by each department. Increasing revenues may be more important to the finance department than savings in time, while a service-oriented department may value savings in time and increased productivity more than increased revenues. Maintaining an advantage over competitors could be the best business case for integrating GIS into an organization as businesses compete for their share of the marketplace.

An organization or business must understand three things to make the most of a GIS investment: (1) the definition of a GIS, (2) the importance of having a commitment to GIS, and (3) the concept of an enterprise GIS.

Custom management tool benefits entire organization

GIS technology is unique because it is both an applied science and a computer-based system. From a technological standpoint, a GIS is an organized collection of computer hardware, software, geographic data, and personnel that efficiently captures, stores, updates, manipulates, analyzes, and displays all forms of geographically referenced information.

From a business perspective, a GIS is a management tool designed to increase both organizational and personal efficiency and productivity. This tool improves decision support, resulting in policies and procedures that save time, increase accuracy, save money, generate revenue, aid in budgeting, automate work flows, and improve resource management. As an organization's GIS program progresses, benefits mount rapidly, and the GIS becomes the institution's information base.

Commitment to GIS

Successful implementation of GIS requires an institutional commitment that extends beyond establishing an ongoing funding mechanism and dedicating personnel resources. The investment requires an organization to educate its employees about the importance of geography in their lives.

Managers must address the technical aspects of the implementation, such as systems design and delivery, but they should also devise a plan that accounts for the human elements of adopting the technology, such as work practices and performance. Organizations should encourage employees to apply spatial reasoning to their work processes and problems. The following checklist can establish a foundation for the organization to achieve maximum returns on the GIS investment:

- Perform a needs assessment. Ask people which tasks they perform in the course of their work.
- Recognize GIS as a competitive advantage.
- Work toward an enterprise implementation.
- Recognize that there are both tangible and intangible benefits.
- Position the GIS to serve all departments to maximize the return on investment and build an effective case to demonstrate GIS accountability and performance measurements across the agency or business.
- Develop common data sets that support the most disciplines. Noting patterns in data requirements for individual departments can help structure the GIS layers to benefit the most users. By identifying opportunities for improvement, issues, and obstacles to overcome, the GIS foundation becomes stronger and more capable of serving as a knowledge base for the entire organization.
- Apply GIS to the work flow as opposed to looking for problems GIS can solve.
- Empower employees to use GIS.

Technology will continue to change the way we live and work, and the capabilities of GIS will expand as new technologies emerge.

Definition of an enterprise implementation

An assessment can provide guidance on how GIS can help. The assessment should identify where an organization can apply GIS to departmental work procedures. This often yields successful GIS applications for specific projects. GIS applications can truly become an enterprise-wide network and yield the maximum return on investment if the process is expanded to observe where department activities overlap with other departments. Establishing a common or centralized data repository from which all departments can draw and build their own spatial awareness and applications is the most effective way to achieve a timely rate of return.

The needs assessment process will help identify areas where GIS can provide support. To avoid pitfalls in interpreting a needs assessment, try to fit GIS into the existing work flow rather than look for individual problems that a GIS can solve.

An enterprise implementation is an organization-wide integration of GIS. An "adaptive enterprise" refers to the process an organization uses to build spatial awareness throughout the group. Adopting an adaptive enterprise approach to GIS rather than a department-by-department implementation leads to the rapid acceptance of a societal approach to extending spatial technologies. An enterprise approach can include Internet-based applications where organization-to-public, employee-to-employee, government-to-government, and government-to-business usage increases the number of GIS users and the benefits realized.

The enterprise redefined is the constant process of questioning how GIS can apply to a business problem or work flow and how to best extend the concepts, data sources, and analytical capabilities as they present themselves. ⊙

An enterprise success in Canada

SECTOR *Enterprise GIS*
INDUSTRY *Government (International)*
Candice Foster
Manager, GIS Services
Regional Municipality of Durham, Ontario, Canada
www.region.durham.on.ca

The Regional Municipality of Durham (Durham Region) is situated in the highly developed and populated economic center of Ontario known as the Golden Horseshoe. With a population of more than 530,000, Durham Region lies immediately to the east of Toronto within the Greater Toronto Area encompassing approximately 2,590 square kilometers. Durham Region comprises a series of major lakeshore urban communities and a variety of small towns, villages, hamlets, and farms that lie immediately inland. The relatively flat lakeshore area, marked by bluffs, wooded creeks, and ancient shoreline, contrasts with the hummocks of the Oak Ridges Moraine that run parallel to the shoreline twenty-five kilometers to the north.

The development of an enterprise GIS has helped Durham Region carry out its mission.

The Regional Municipality of Durham formed in 1974 and includes the cities of Oshawa and Pickering; the towns of Ajax and Whitby; the municipality of Clarington; and the townships of Brock, Scugog, and Uxbridge. Durham Region and its eight area municipalities work together to respond to the challenges of a diverse and growing area. Durham Region's mission is to provide safe, efficient, and effective services that protect the environment, support the development of healthy and prosperous communities, and reflect the diverse and changing needs of its citizens and customers.

The development of an enterprise GIS has helped Durham Region carry out its mission. Durham Region began implementing GIS in November 2001, when the Corporate Strategic Plan identified the technology as a strategic priority. The GIS implementation resulted from the development of a GIS strategy and a five-year implementation plan developed in conjunction with all departments in Durham Region.

Public Works, Planning, and a few other Durham Region departments had small-scale GIS programs before the implementation of the corporate GIS philosophy. The organization used several different software platforms and GIS data standards but lacked coordination between the groups. The departments not using GIS conducted their business manually.

As part of Durham Region's GIS strategy, the Corporate GIS Services Department officially formed in October 2001 within the Corporate Information Services Department. It consists of a manager, a senior GIS specialist, and two GIS specialists. During the development of the GIS strategy, Durham Region determined that the department would be the best place for GIS to meet the needs of all departments. During the early stages, Durham Region's success depended on a tight link between GIS and the traditional IT functions, such as those

In Ottawa, Canada, regional planners carry out their mission with the help of GIS. This enterprise-wide implementation gives all regional departments and external partners easy access to data and applications. The map shows the location of a school under construction and the residents within four hundred meters who may be affected by the noise.

of the database administrators, programmers, and network administrators.

The Corporate Information Services Department coordinates the organization's GIS activities. These include installing and configuring the software and developing applications, maintaining the operation and development of the corporate GIS, developing and maintaining GIS and related standards and procedures, providing GIS expertise and assisting departments in the use of the corporate GIS, conducting performance and tuning checks to ensure the system is running smoothly and efficiently, providing all of the spatial database administration services, ensuring upgrades and patches are implemented, and identifying each department's responsibilities and data access levels and rights, which are approved by executive management.

The Corporate Information Services Department maintains the core land base data layers including the single line road network, parcel fabric,

and orthophotography. It also manages the relationship and integration of data from external providers such as vendors, other public sector organizations including the Ministry of Natural Resources, local municipalities, conservation authorities, and utilities.

"GIS has significantly changed the way business processes within our organization are organized and managed," said Candice Foster, manager of GIS Services. "Departments now centrally store all of their GIS data in the geodatabase and are able to maintain the data from their offices. Updates and corrections are completed daily by Durham Region's departments as well as the external data providers, and since the database is dynamic, users are able to see the changes right away. The geodatabase allows all GIS data assets to be consolidated and shared across the organization, which eliminates silos and duplication of effort." ➢

MAP LEGEND
Distance from Park
Buffer Distance
■ 0 - 60m
■ 60 - 120m
□ 120 - 180m
• Residential Building
■ Com./Indust./Inst. Building
■ Forested Area
—+— Railway

ArcGIS maps were created to notify residents of
a municipal festival taking place in a local park.

Durham Region developed an ArcIMS Intranet Mapping and GIS Engine (I.M.A.G.E.) as a main application available to all staff. This viewer provides users with live access to data stored in the centralized geodatabase and the ability to export and print maps for reports and presentations, query attribute data, buffer, hyperlink to photographs and images, and measure distances. ArcSDE and the geodatabase provide a centralized mechanism for managing and

sharing geographic data in a relational database management system.

GIS has been available to all departments since May 2002, and currently fifteen hundred users have access to the Web-based GIS to use the geodatabase's more than sixty layers. Generally, this group uses I.M.A.G.E. to query, buffer, perform analysis, and produce custom maps.

The more advanced ArcGIS users access the geodatabase for specialized purposes such as updating data and performing advanced spatial analysis and mapping. Many of Durham Region's departments, including Legal, Public Works, Police Services, and Housing Services, use GIS for such things as maps for committee meetings, surveying, analysis, reporting, and dissemination of information.

"GIS enables me to provide departmental and regional staff and the public with up-to-date information regarding rent-geared-to-income housing projects within Durham Region including nearest major intersection, local elementary and high schools for both the public and separate school boards, places of worship, transit, and local medical facilities," said Sherry J. Lee–Cockburn, administrative support, Housing Services. "With GIS we can personalize our service by enabling clients to view areas of the region they are unfamiliar with and the amenities available, which is an extremely important factor when applying for housing."

Durham Region's Long-Term Care and Services for Seniors Division (Social Services) staff use I.M.A.G.E. and ArcView to access the corporate ArcSDE/Oracle geodatabase for a combination of corporate and long-term, care-specific data such as census data and population projections.

"We have had access to GIS for ten months and have found it to be quite useful," said Liz Dowie, manager of Information Technology, Long-Term Care and Services for Seniors Division. "We use ArcView to illustrate the location of long-term care facilities, adult day programs, and medical centers. It helps us see a clear image of our demographic catchment areas and establish trends to show where more long-term care facilities may be required in the future."

Durham Region's Health Services Department staff also accesses the geodatabase via I M A G E and ArcView. The staff uses ArcView to track West Nile virus findings including dead bird cases, infected human cases, and mosquito larvae breeding sites. The geodatabase is used to present West Nile information to the appropriate stakeholders including the Public Health Department.

Durham Region's Economic Development Department is developing a map-based online business directory using ArcIMS, an ArcGIS application used to track available industrial land for local governments and industry. There is also an ArcIMS Web-based tourism portal for Durham Region developed with GeoSmart funding from the Ontario government.

The Durham Emergency Measures Office is building data layers for emergency response in what-if scenarios and emergency exercises. The Corporate GIS Services Department is participating in emergency exercises to analyze situations and assist with

GIS has been available to all departments since May 2002, and currently fifteen hundred users have access to the Web-based GIS to use the geodatabase's more than sixty layers.

information to determine the best course of action. The Corporate GIS staff participates in emergency and planning exercises involving multilevel organizations and partnerships to ensure everyone has the most accurate and up to date information. The exercises include live GIS analysis, such as nuclear planning to assist in critical decision making about resident safety and the best course of action to take.

Moving forward

Durham Region is continuing to follow the five-year implementation plan through 2006. The vision provides regional departments and external partners with easier access to data and applications and to GIS to increase public service levels for constituents. Durham Region plans to make many of the data and tools currently used internally available to the public via a GIS Internet portal. This portal will provide access to GIS layers, tools for theme specific analysis, digital maps in PDF format, and the ability to query public resources such as government sites, tourism information, and property neighborhood information. ⊙

ADDITIONAL BENEFITS

Town's vision reaps many rewards

SECTOR *Enterprise GIS*
INDUSTRY *Government*

Todd Jackson
GIS Manager, City of Westerville, Ohio
www.ci.westerville.oh.us

The fundamental role of government is to provide optimized services to its constituents—from economic development to planning and zoning to law enforcement to schools to public works and utilities. Municipalities today benefit from technology to automate, streamline, and maximize service delivery. GIS is poised to play a key role in the evolution of government. Forward-thinking cities, such as Westerville, Ohio, a fast growing suburb of Columbus, use enterprise GIS networks to connect all areas of their government infrastructure, ensuring the best service possible for their constituents.

"We've grown from a GIS in one or two departments in 1999 to a full enterprise GIS," said Todd Jackson, Westerville GIS manager. "We've evolved from departmental GIS to enterprise GIS, and now it's extending to the community. We've done a lot, and there's potential still to be realized."

An Ohio tradition

For nearly two hundred years, Westerville has maintained a rich tradition of friendliness and quality of life. As central Ohio's largest suburb, Westerville's thirty-seven thousand residents benefit from its many services—the most of any central Ohio suburb. The city has more than 150 trained full-time police officers and firefighters, an electric division, a water division recognized as one of the state's finest, and a state-of-the-art community center. Westerville maintains approximately sixty spatial data layers, not counting the Electric Division.

In 1995, the city's information systems manager began researching automated software packages that could replace time-consuming manual methods for producing paper maps of city infrastructure. In 2000, the city's GIS staff, as part of the technology evaluation process, met with city employees in each department to explain how GIS could help them in their daily tasks. City staff learned how GIS could

Three-dimensional mapping capabilities helps with land-use planning.

not only automate map production but could also function as an advanced analysis tool. Furthermore, an enterprise database environment that facilitated advanced query, analysis, and visualization could manage a wealth of information.

"When we were looking at current GIS packages, we interviewed different department staff to see what they wanted and how we could best serve their needs," said Jackson. "We liked ESRI's enterprise approach, and we liked the future direction of the technology." Initially, Westerville acquired GIS to automate maps and map production in the planning department. Soon the city realized the value of GIS analysis capabilities.

Westerville now implements the full gamut of ESRI tools—ArcPad, ArcView, ArcEditor™, ArcInfo, ArcSDE, ArcIMS, ArcReader™, and ArcGIS Publisher. Ten departments use GIS, and approximately

Ten departments use GIS, and approximately three hundred city staff members have access to GIS tools via the intranet.

three hundred city staff members have access to GIS tools via the intranet. During 2002, between the internal and external Web sites, an average of twenty thousand map requests were made each month.

"For the size of the community we have, we're getting a lot of map requests," said Jackson. "People like the functionality of the software and the accessibility to different data sets. With the intuitive interface, both public users and internal city staff are using more geospatial information than ever for their various decision-making processes." ➤

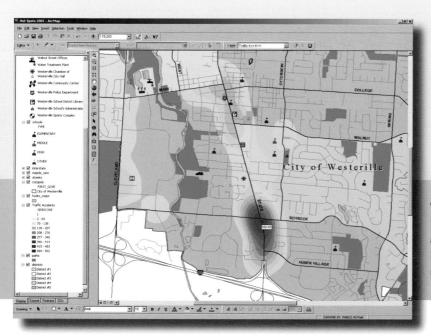

With the help of GIS, Westerville, Ohio, has automated map production, analysis, and work flows in many departments including law enforcement, utilities, school redistricting, planning, and assessment.

Diverse uses in crime analysis, utilities, and schools

GIS made an immediate impact in law enforcement. Burglaries, robberies, sex crimes, and other major incidents are input into the GIS database, which crime analyst Lt. Al Kolp uses to discover crime patterns.

"That's just one example where the analysis and display capabilities helped us do our jobs more effectively." — Lt. Al Kolp

"We were getting hit terribly at doctor's offices, pharmacies, day care centers, and other similar business types," said Kolp. "We performed detailed spatial analysis and were able to pinpoint an exact time frame and location. We notified personnel when and where to pay particular attention and included a detailed map. A task force was created, and the second week after we set it up we caught the perpetrators. That's just one example where the analysis and display capabilities helped us do our jobs more effectively." A similar analysis helped with car break-ins.

Crime analysts also mapped traffic accident hot spots to help law enforcement officers spot traffic violations. "If we can perform analysis and find the hot spots for any number of particular crimes, then we can better deploy our resources," said Kolp.

Westerville's Electric Division uses GIS in every aspect of its operation. The former CAD-only shop now manages approximately twenty-five intelligent spatial data layers integrated with volumes of tabular information.

The city uses GIS to perform work order management, facilities management, and construction planning. The division is currently implementing ArcFM™ Energy from Miner & Miner, Consulting Engineers, Inc., of Fort Collins, Colorado, for tabular and vector data creation, maintenance, and manipulation. The city uses ArcPad to perform in-field asset management that is uploaded into the enterprise GIS. Linemen use GIS data for trouble call analysis. Customer billing and load information is available to phone operators who can quickly scan information for service calls. In addition, the city uses GIS to produce map books that provide greater information detail and data updates for the entire city electric system.

"We're always adding new facilities, and GIS gives us a better way to manage and update information and to perform analysis," said Guy Precht, electric GIS/CAD technician. "The technology foundation is especially appealing. It's like building a house. You're never completely satisfied, and you're always looking for ways to improve. As new functionality is added, we're able to do more and better things with the software."

For school redistricting, city staff did a better job reformatting school zones by using different data analysis and visualization techniques. Staff also better communicated its reasoning for the new school zones. The Westerville City School District is ninth largest in the state with more than fourteen thousand students.

"In the past we'd use colored pencils and paper maps," said Dr. Mary Peters, director of Assessment and Planning, Westerville City School District. "We turned to GIS for a number of reasons. We wanted the redistricting process to be more efficient, visual,

Maps help communities provide input on planned developments, which are quickly mapped and visually accessed for feasiblity.

and accurate; ensure equity among schools and across the district; and make the entire process interactive between the community and the school district."

The nine-month project time frame enabled community members and the school board to weigh many variables before finalizing redistricting plans. It also provided for constant community input and creation of new school zone possibilities. When new plans were proposed, data was quickly mapped and visually assessed for feasibility.

"GIS is a technology that more school boards need to learn about," said Peters. "It's tremendous for all kinds of planning efforts, and because of its visualization capabilities, we were able to work better with citizens. All sides benefited." The redistricting process created more than just a product. It implemented a decision-making process using the school data in conjunction with the city's enterprise and community GIS.

The GIS group

Westerville's GIS Group is responsible for developing policies and procedures for GIS system updates and providing project management, support, maintenance, and implementation of the citywide GIS. The group distributes desktop GIS to all city users whose work requires spatial data integration and analysis of spatial and tabular data. Its members instruct city departments and the community on what GIS is and how they can apply GIS to their existing business practices and work flows. Maintaining a working relationship with all departments, department heads, and users is also a priority. The department defines the direction and manages the growth of the GIS for Westerville, based on user needs and the overall technology strategy within Westerville. ➤

The GIS department maintains base information. Parcels, centerlines, and other data are acquired from Delaware and Franklin counties and merged to create a seamless basemap for the city. Departments build their information on top of the basemap. Users throughout the city can then view and access all data. A utility user can see when the streets department plans to dig up and repave a road and can schedule underground facilities maintenance around the single road construction activity.

A mapping icon enables citizens visiting the city Web site at *www.westerville.org* to pan and zoom throughout the city while viewing parcel and other information. They can also access the mapping functionality through the economic development Web page. They can perform queries based on address, parcel identification numbers, or landmarks. Users can pick and choose a variety of data layers including schools, interstates, major roads, streets, water, and parks. In addition, they can access aerial photography, zoning, and links to Franklin and Delaware parcel tax mapping.

"We're still working to get some departments not involved with GIS actively using the tools," said Jackson. "We'd like to expand the enterprise GIS concept to include other community stakeholders, for instance, Otterbein College, St. Anne Hospital, and the Westerville Chamber of Commerce. We have a platform that fulfills needs now and is scalable for the future."

In 2002, the city of Westerville received an ESRI Special Achievement in GIS Award for its successful enterprise GIS program. ◉

"We've grown from a GIS in one or two departments in 1999 to a full enterprise GIS."

Todd Jackson

ADDITIONAL BENEFITS

GIS returns on its investment

GIS has evolved into a mainstream technology because, for the organizations and businesses that use GIS, it continues to yield a return on the investment. Quantifiable benefits include time saved to perform a task, costs avoided or money saved, revenue generated or recovered, and increased productivity and accuracy. Other key payoffs include decision support, increased efficiency, and increased communication.

The system works better when organizations implement an enterprise-wide system that connects geography to the business process. With online services, such as interactive mapping, agencies can better serve citizens, businesses are enhanced, and internal government operations—IT infrastructure, data management and warehousing, information exchange, and field force automation—are more efficient and flexible.

Measuring the benefits of GIS

Data creation and maintenance sets the foundation for moving forward with a successful GIS. A strategy of thorough documentation and criteria analysis, coupled with recent breakthroughs in GIS software that enable Web-deployed applications, is paving the way for organizations as they aggressively strive to provide more efficient and effective services and products.

As these processes move forward and more GIS applications are put into use, GIS users will look for ways to identify and document how GIS technology benefits their organizations and their customers and how they can add to their return on investment by integrating GIS into other business work flows. Reflecting on how these business tasks would be accomplished without a GIS can bring to mind many of its benefits.

Continuously measuring the benefits of GIS can be contagious, and organizations and businesses will begin to find new ways of calculating and tracking benefits and exceeding those benefits each year. Users, managers, and public officials will recognize the benefits and business value of GIS to justify continued investments in GIS.

The future promises that the benefits of GIS will be measured with more sophisticated and powerful formulas enabling us to identify more advantages for all. Measuring the benefits of GIS will positively transform organizations into more effective and successful operations.

To learn more about the benefits of GIS or to submit your own benefits of GIS case study, visit *www.esri.com/measuringbenefits.*

organization index